COUNSELLING TRAUMA and RELIGION

Counselling the Sexually Abused

By E. McCreave

Cover painting: Michael McKernon

Published by The Shanway Press, Belfast 2006

ISBN: 0-9543906-4-4   978-0-9543906-4-8

Cover painting: Michael McKernon

Published by Shanway Press, Belfast 2006

www.shanway.com

Designed and printed by Shanway Press.

Typeset in New Century Schoolbook.

Acknowledgement: The material in this book that was based
on the article, *'The Future of Trauma Work'* as it appeared in
*CPJ (Counselling and Psychotherapy Journal), May 2004, Vol
15, No 1,* is printed with the kind permission of the British
Association for Counselling and Psychotherapy (BACP).

Copies may be acquired via our website:

www.shanway.com

ISBN: 0-9543906-4-4   978-0-9543906-4-8

To the memory of my parents, Bob and Theresa

The way to humanise the system
is to reject equality
and to cherish the individual case.

- *Mary Douglas, Natural Symbols, 1970*

Contents

Preface

Media attention on child sexual abuse has had one unexpected consequence; it has reminded many individuals of their own childhood abuse. And while there certainly has been a rise in the number of people seeking compensation through litigation, it seems likely that a lot more have been quietly going to counsellors in order to cope with their distress. Of these, some may have been referred by their doctors. But it seems more likely that many, influenced by media reports of adult 'victims' being referred to 'appropriate professional counsellors', may have sought such help on their own initiative.

The question, of course, is: what's an 'appropriate professional counsellor'? Is s/he one who has been appropriately trained to be a counsellor? Or is s/he one who has been appropriately trained to work with the traumatic effects of former sexual abuse? The media does not make a distinction between the former 'counsellor' and the latter 'trauma counsellor', nor does the public realise that there is one. As a result, many counsellors are finding themselves in the position - not unlike that faced by clergy - of having to deal with a topic in which they have had little to no training.

Ordinarily, counsellors are familiar with the

characteristics of a helper as defined by Carl Rogers. Many are equally familiar with the counselling *process* as described by Gerard Egan. All are capable of working from this background in a variety of situations by simply adapting to them. For instance, as a result of having received further training and essential information, they can move into, say, counselling the bereaved, counselling those with AIDS, counselling those with cancer, marriage counselling etc.

The danger is, as I see it, that many counsellors will assume that the same arrangement should apply when working with the sexually abused. They will work under the illusion that what is required is information about the traumatic effects of abuse, information which will help them to better understand a client who previously had been abused as a child.

At least, that is what I assumed when I began to counsel over thirty years ago. But in those days, nobody knew much about psychological trauma and its effects. And in Northern Ireland where I worked, there did not seem to be anyone else to whom I could refer such 'victims' of abuse. Indeed, counselling itself seemed to be an unknown entity back then. As a result, I resorted to my own training in counselling (under an early student of Carl Rogers), and on my experience of psychoanalysis (under a Neo-Freudian, medical practitioner), both in the States and in the mid-60s; if nothing else, I was fairly sure that I would not do much harm!

Over the subsequent years, I have learned quite a lot, not only from my clients but also from the first books about trauma that began to appear in the '80s. Still, I was aware that the latter focused either on symptoms if written by psychiatrists, or behaviour if written by psychologists, but that none seemed to refer to the 'talking therapies' as such. This left me wondering what it was that counsellors could do to facilitate abused people who sought their help.

Now retired, I thought it might help younger counsellors if I described what I've learned over the years. If nothing else it might help in distinguishing between a 'counsellor' and a 'trauma counsellor'. That difference, as already mentioned, is not one of adaptation but of orientation. In other words, when dealing with an abused client, counsellors not only must recognise the symptoms of trauma, but also must *change their attitudes and their very approach to such clients*. It is this radical re-orientation that makes dealing with trauma quite different from almost all other forms of counselling. I hope this will become clearer as we move through this book.

Working on the text has been a learning experience for me. Like most counsellors, I normally focus on what I do and rarely have reason or opportunity to reflect on how I do it. Only when I sit at a computer to write for someone else, am I able to contemplate this latter point. As a result, I am now clearer in mind, and can say that it was not intuition - or not just intuition - but also the coming together of different strands in my life that made me the counsellor I am today.

Those strands came together like threads on the loom to weave a pattern that I saw – as surely as I can hear three of the notes in a musical chord but am unable to teach others how to harmonise naturally. It made sense to put them in writing in the hope that they might be of use to others. Or maybe it would be better to say that I have teased apart the tapestry and am now in a better position to describe the strands of thought that formed the pattern.

In other words, when you read this book you will find that one of the threads involves paradigms (archetypes or models), another ties in the counselling theories of Rogers and Egan, another describes the nature of the social world, another the influence of war, another the nature of communication, another the nature of myth and fairytales, yet another the roles of men and women in society etc. I have pulled these apart before the blank screen of my computer, and then tried to weave them together into a more coherent form when typing this final script.

I appreciate that you, the reader, will be more interested in *how* to counsel the abused than in *why* an approach such as I use is required. However, and especially when dealing with the sexually abused, you as counsellor are dealing with someone who has been exposed to **evil;** you are moving into an area that psychologists and counsellors tend to either deny or avoid, given its association with religion.

Accordingly, you will understand if I attempt to slow down any approach to counselling the abused by first considering what happened in the States when counselling principles were applied to groups in which evil also appeared. It will take some time for you to grasp the connection between this initial material and counselling the sexually abused. But for me, it is fairly basic to any understanding of why counsellors simply have to change their core stance when dealing with a client who had been sexually abused as a child. Unlike regular counsellors who have to deal with wisdom and behaviour, trauma counsellors (or 'psychological counsellors' as they are now referred to in the States) have to deal with a socio-religious phenomenon as I hope to show in this work.

You will also notice that I say little in this book about sexual abusers. And when I do, I invariably refer to them in masculine terms, a stance entirely in keeping with the popular myth that most abusers are male. Still, it is worth keeping in mind that the sexual abuse of children is by no means limited to one sex only! I merely use the masculine form for the sake of convenience.

Finally, what I write may not be sufficient, but I believe that it certainly is necessary.

Introduction

The title of this book, *Counselling, Trauma and Religion*, requires some explanation before going further.

Counselling

By *counselling* I mean the process of personal reorientation by which someone discovers new self-understanding, integration and better ways of behaving. It is distinct from *guidance*, the process of supplying the person with information pertinent to a specific situation. And it differs from *teaching*, the process of supplying the person with information needed in a variety of situations. In more recent times, counselling has become associated with *therapy* to the extent that it is now difficult to distinguish it from psychotherapy.

In this book, I limit myself to the helping processes designed by Carl R. Rogers and Gerard Egan, the two most widely known figures in the general field of counselling. Both came from Chicago, Illinois, the birthplace of modern counselling.

Trauma

By trauma I mean the after-affects of a shock arising from either a near-death experience, or the sudden and unexpected breaking of attachment bonds. The after-affects are both medical and psychological. They are also social and spiritual. The combination makes for complications in their treatment. For the medical dimension, I am indebted to Judith Lewis Herman, Bessel van der Kolk and Sandra Bloom, in short, to the Harvard Medical School and its students.

Religion

By religion I mean the relationship between humanity and God. While not excluding the well-known religions of our modern world, I focus primarily on the ancient roots of all religions – the archaic forms that only survive today in remote and primitive societies. In the study of these I am indebted primarily to Mircea Eliade, Professor of Comparative Religions at the University of Chicago.

The common link, then, between counselling, trauma and religion is their mutual interest in order and opposition to disorder. As I hope to show, counselling deals with the disorders that people experience on a personal level, trauma is a consequence of either a social or natural disorder, while religion explains where our understanding of order came from in the first place - and can even be useful in its restoration.

Speaking of disorder, it is possible for someone who reads this book to conclude that I am opposed to Carl Rogers and his counselling principles. If so, let me categorically state that I have both taught his theories for over 30 years and made use of them as a counsellor for even longer. I am convinced of the effectiveness of his approach in a one-to-one counselling situation.

What concerns me is, not his counselling principles as such, but the misinterpretation of them by others, by any application of those principles outside of the counselling room or in a social setting, and by his rather paradoxical attitude towards authority (he was an author who opposed authority!) These are some of the dangers that I highlight in the coming chapters. However, in my approach, I say little about the earlier part of his academic career (with which counsellors will already be familiar), and limit myself to material from his later career with encounter groups (with which most counsellors will be less familiar). As a consequence, a bias towards the negative will appear that can lead to an unbalanced conclusion in the minds of those unfamiliar with the beneficial results of Rogers' earlier work. While unfortunate for the casual reader, it was not altogether unintentional with regards to counsellors; I wanted the latter to know that if the founder of modern counselling 'took a wrong turn' - as I believe he did when opting to move from counselling to encounter groups - then it is equally possible for them to do likewise should they apply Rogers' principles outside of a counselling setting e.g. in their families or any other social grouping. And I especially wanted counsellors to know the danger in applying regular counselling principles to an adult client previously traumatised by child sex abuse.

1. BEGINNINGS

1. Paradigms

Karl Menninger, an American psychiatrist, once wrote a book called, *"Whatever Became of Sin?"* In this he noted that there are three professions - the priest, the doctor, and the police - which once were one. All evolved from the ancient Temple priests who opposed evil in all its forms – spiritual, physical, and social – and who cured the soul, healed the body and guarded the community's moral standards. Today, the priest opposes sin, the doctor opposes sickness, and the police oppose crime.

What bothered Menninger was, not that these professions had a common ancestor, but they had a common tendency to use each other's language; for example, when a bomb exploded in N. Ireland, the clergy were liable to say, "Whoever did that committed a terrible *crime!*" while the police might say, "Whoever did that must have been *sick!*" Accordingly, he as a doctor wondered if the medical profession should add, "Whoever did that committed a *sin!*" (Hence the title of his book, *"Whatever Became of Sin?"*) Menninger then recommended that each profession should adhere to its own terminology.

Implied in the above is that all modern professions which oppose evil - therapists, psychoanalysts, psychologists, psychiatrists, lawyers, judges, police etc - operate from the paradigm (archetype, model or blue-print from which something is built) of The Priest. This means that, just as the priest once carried out certain rituals in the Temple in an impersonal way, so professionals (who deal with sickness and crime) now use rituals in the State. And as the laity then had access to God through the priest despite the latter's personal flaws and vices, so too the public now have access to health and justice through professionals despite their personal flaws and vices. In other words, the original *impersonal* behaviour of the priest in the Temple became the model for later professionals in the State.

There is, however, another paradigm that still carries influence today – that of The Wise One. After the Temple of the Old Testament was first destroyed some 2500 years ago, a new class of laity arose to keep alive the readings of The Bible. These were initially the scribes (on whose writing skills international businessmen depended for long-distance communication), later the businessmen themselves.

On the international trade routes, these merchants had come across the *wisdom*, as it was called, of the Egyptians and Greeks. The arts of wisdom had been developed by the business class in those countries as a way of surviving in a hostile world. You could always tell a wise man by how rich he was and by how old he was; any man who could hang on to his money when surrounded by kings and brigands, all out to tax or rob him, had to have a secret to his success; any man who could live a long life when surrounded by relatives, eager to get their hands on his wealth, and prepared to damage his health in the process, had to have a secret to his success. In short, any man who could, "Live long and prosper" - like Mr Spock of Star Trek - had to have an extra card or two up his sleeve.

Parents, who wanted their sons to learn those secrets, apprenticed them to such men at a time when there were no schools. In turn, businessmen did what they still do today; they used *commercials* to get their message across. They taught their wisdom by using short, sharp statements that could easily be remembered: "*A bird in the hand is worth two in the bush*", "*A rolling stone gathers no moss*" etc. In short, they taught through proverbs.

The Hebrew merchants, who had returned home with this pagan wisdom, soon realised that The Bible they read to the people also contained the secret of a wealthy and healthy life – keep the Commandments! If anything, their Hebrew wisdom was even older that that of the pagans! It was just a matter of time before they began to add their own reflections to The Bible; we know these as the Books of Wisdom and Proverbs.

It is also worth noting that merchants in those days depended heavily on luck when engaging in international trade. Even soldiers needed luck since they too were in a risky business; it is not surprising that they took up gambling as a way to pass the time when not fighting; both soldiers and businessmen gambled at work, so why not when at leisure? In either case, luck was important. And to get luck, all turned to gods and lucky stars in the hope of being blessed by good fortune (it was a star that led three Wise Men to Bethlehem). This interest in the heavens paved the way for the development of astronomy and theology as the first sciences. Consequently, the wise men of old became the paradigm or model for later scientists, bookmakers, teachers, businessmen, stock-brokers, accountants, politicians, civil servants, etc. in short, for all engaged in a search, for those who took a risk to reach a goal, and for all whose final output would be carefully examined by others.

In summary, then, the paradigm of Priest is used by

those who deal with *evil* (anything that diminishes the possibility of good), while the paradigm of Wise One is used by those who deal with *risk* (anything that increases the possibility of harm).

In the light of all this, a question arises as to which paradigm lies behind counselling? Do counsellors function as Wise One or Priest? I think the answer is quite clear and unequivocal; counselling has been associated with *wisdom* for over two thousand years; it deals with the question of how to reduce the element of *risk* by increasing the *odds or chances* of success when working towards a goal. Even today, experts like Krumboltz of Stanford University maintain that counselling deals with two issues – and only two issues; how to make a *wise* decision, and how to change inappropriate behaviour. Traditionally, counsellors have always operated from the model of Wise One.

However, there can be little doubt that modern counselling has undergone a change in paradigm. Instead of maintaining its link with education and business, counselling has gradually become one of the talking *therapies*. The latter, of course, is a medical term. And, as indicated above, the medical world and its therapists work from the paradigm of Priest in opposing the evil of ill health. Indeed, counsellors - be they therapists or otherwise - are even expected by today's society to cope with the medical consequences of social evils such as child sexual abuse!

But perhaps it may be more accurate to state that while some counsellors follow the paradigm of the Wise One, others follow that of The Priest. This may explain why the British Association of Counselling had so much difficulty when trying to identify exactly who were counsellors - and ended up presenting a wide spectrum that ranged from psychotherapists (Priest) at one end of the scale, to advice-givers (Wise One) at the other end, and with most counsellors falling somewhere in between, apparently trying to use both paradigms at the same time!

Currently, the situation may seem a little confused – and confusing – but I believe that an evolutionary process is taking place, and that any changes in our understanding of counselling merely reflect similar changes taking place in the environment.

2. The evolution of modern counselling

Back in the early days, Carl Rogers and his students at the University of Chicago had carried out research into the characteristics of a helper that clients had found beneficial. By developing those characteristics, they created a new form of helping and called it *counselling*. It was first used in a university setting to help college students - especially those from small High Schools in rural areas - adjust to a large city and an equally large campus. As a consequence, counselling was viewed initially as a form of education; it had been designed to help students whose anxieties were interfering with their capacity *to learn*.

From a university setting, counselling next moved into U.S. High Schools and, eventually, to Grade Schools (primary schools in our part of the world). Again, it continued to be educational in nature.

The first major change of direction for counselling began when it was introduced to the parents of those same children as *Marriage Counselling*. This paved the way for its moving into other areas entirely unrelated to education - although, for a while, it continued to be seen by some academics as the property of the Department of Education for teaching purposes, while others thought it belonged to the Department of Psychology. Rogers, of course, continued to speak about himself and his counsellors as 'learners', an educational term.

Even the terms *counsellor and client* were adaptations

of the educational *student and teacher*; counsellors took-on the role of *student* in the working relationship, while encouraging clients *to teach* them all about themselves (the general idea was that the only one who learned anything in a classroom was the teacher!   If so, perhaps if clients lectured the counsellor on their favourite topic - themselves - they too might learn something! And, naturally, counsellors responded like students in class; they summarised and gave back to the client-as-teacher the latter's own material, asking, "Am I following you correctly?")

A further development took place once counsellors sought *employment* in educational settings. A question arose as to whether they were members of staff or not. If they were, then why employ outside staff when current teachers could double as counsellors in their own school? If not, then what was the relationship between in-coming counsellors and the school administration? Such questions were critical since it was important to clarify the counsellor's status in the system. Did the counsellor work for the administration or for the client?

The final decision appears to have been based on psychological facts, not opinions. The simple fact was - and still is - that all systems are *masculine* by their very nature (they operate from the pyramid model with the boss at the top, not from the feminine model of a circle with the leader in the centre); it makes no difference whether they are run by men or women. Once you join a system, you *always* work for the person above you, not for those below. For example, a teacher in a school is employed to take care of the principal, not the students, a concept taken from the military, the model that all systems follow. In the army, there are at least two classes below the general: the foot-soldiers who have to be given orders, and the officer class - or 'gentlemen' - whose job it is *to know what the general wants before the general knows he wants it.*

The reason for acting in this way is because systems work like an army at war. And in times of war, decision-making has to be centralised to ensure a swift response to danger. This explains why officers, at a meeting called by the general, present *necessary facts* but hide their opinions; they only give him what he needs/wants to hear – his own views (any sharing of different opinions would take time and, in any case, would only confuse the general). The same is true of business systems, social systems, political and health systems etc. All function along the lines of a military machine such as the ancient Roman Army.

What was clearly missing in this macho world was the presence of the *feminine*. Such an absence became acutely felt in an educational system that involved children. For while the use of drugs to combat stress was a not-infrequent occurrence in other systems during the '60s, it simply was not an option for children; clearly, they needed a mother figure to support them in times of stress. Accordingly, counsellors were first introduced to the school in this capacity. Again, it made no difference whether the counsellors were female or male; their function was the same – to take care of the children as a mother would; their task was to *understand* the students more than supply them with guidance (the latter is the job of teachers).

The implications, however, were revolutionary. For the first time, a system was introducing a non-system person whose function was to take care of those *below her* in the hierarchy. While employed by the system, she did not work for the system. Rather, she was there to support the child, not the school's standards. If anything, she was to the principal what a mother is to a father in the family, someone who does not work *for* - but stands *beside* - him, while sharing a mutual responsibility for the children (by way of analogy, such a figure in parliament is the loyal opposition, someone who attacks the government but is not anti-government). This family concept of shared power or dual authority so as to create a balance makes complete sense if you think about it, but at the time was entirely novel when applied to systems.

For one thing, it meant that a teacher could not be a counsellor in the same school; as I said before, all teachers are employed to take care of the principal, not the students. All represent the system and uphold its standards. As such, they form a class apart from counsellors. In fact, the teachers in the Chicago school where I taught in the early '60s never even *met* the counsellors; the latter were 'outsiders' who worked in the school basement (we referred to them as, "The moles"); they had the power to summons a child out of the classroom at any moment, and only informed the principal of the number dealt with over a period of time, not the issues that arose in the counselling sessions. Equally, we teachers referred troubled children to them - not to disciplinarians - for counselling. It resulted in a fairly peaceful school in the black ghetto of Chicago's West Side (at the time, the term 'black' referred to a positive attitude or way of thinking about a racial group, not just to a colour).

Given that the relationship between counsellor and principal was based entirely on mutual trust, the onus was on the principal to ensure - *before employing the counsellor* - that s/he really was both trustworthy and competent! Accordingly, great effort was placed on screening applicants to ensure that their personal characteristics, values and attitudes were as transparent as their level of competence. The screening focused on issues like the impact of religious beliefs on the role of the counsellor, how to care for marginalized clients, client selection, the counsellor's duty of confidentiality and the avoidance of harm, the relationship between counselling principles and religious social thought, religious freedom and freedom of conscience etc.

Inevitably, such screening placed a burden on administrators who wearied and opted for simplistic 'Codes of Ethics' as an alternative. In effect, this was the equivalent of father giving mother a formal Code to ensure that the children were properly cared for in his absence. The paternalism was as transparent as it was appalling. While protecting those in authority in the school, such Codes did little for students, and even less for counsellors who no longer had to examine their own conscience – or even think about it – since adherence to a Code of Ethics was all that mattered. Counsellors, of course, had become amoral practitioners (non-judgemental) as had been Carl Rogers – reinforcing the need for such Codes to begin with.

Equally unfortunate was the effect on counselling; what once had been an esteemed profession associated with education, now began a gradual decline; the original idea of a mother in a family who shared authority *with* her husband, was replaced by that of a human resource manager *under* a captain (as in the TV series, *Star Trek: The Next Generation*) and, finally, degraded to that of a staff-member *under* a line-manager in the system, one who now required training (not education) in counselling as befitted someone of a lower status.

In summary, then, counselling flourished originally when used in an educational setting, but began to decline in stature to the extent that it became a form of therapy for adults. As they moved from the paradigm of Wise One in education to that of Priest along medical lines, counsellors found themselves becoming somewhat begrudged servants in the Temple of Health. Furthermore, the focus was no longer on the development of *wisdom* to facilitate decision-making in the social world, but on the development of *personal characteristics* to facilitate psychological growth and mental health in the individual. And the man who started it all was the psychologist, Carl Rogers.

3. Psychiatry and Psychology

Previously, I said that any profession that deals with *evil* operates from the paradigm of Priest. Clearly, psychologists fall into this category. However, a difficulty arises with humanistic psychologists like Rogers who do not believe in evil to begin with; to them human nature is essentially good, creative and capable of healthy growth. It follows that such psychologists do not follow the paradigm of Priest but, rather, that of Wise One. This is particularly true of Rogers who saw himself as a 'learner'. Furthermore, in the *Gloria tapes*, he even stated that, "Life is a *risky* business", a remark which implies that a psychologist - like a businessman - must learn from his mistakes (or 'experiences' as Rogers called them).

On the other hand, Rogers never called himself a counsellor. Instead, he saw himself primarily as a human being, but would acknowledge that his degree had been in psychology. Still, it would seem that, while Rogers was determined to follow the model of Wise One (or, 'A skilled political animal' as Thorne described him in his book *Carl Rogers; Sage, 1992*), he also had a hidden side that longed to follow the paradigm of Priest – as evidenced by his move after 1957 to working with the evil of schizophrenia, and later with encounter groups in which evil once more appeared (as I will show later).

It suffices at the moment to note that counselling was the child of educational and humanistic psychology, even if it later began to move in the direction of medicine and its psychiatrists as did Rogers. Given this tentative and developing link between psychologists and psychiatrists, it makes sense to first consider the obvious question: what's the difference between these two professions? The answer lies in their different approaches to the human mind.

In general terms, the mind is influenced by two forces – those that lie within the body, and those that lie without. People who study the influence of internal forces (the *body*) on the mind are known as psychiatrists, while those who study the influence of external forces (the *group*) are known as psychologists. This is true in both the U.S. and Europe. But while psychiatrists on both sides of the Atlantic agree on the meaning of a 'body', psychologists have different understandings of what is meant by a 'group'.

The different understandings reflect the differences between American and European Constitutions. That of the U.S. gives rights to individuals whereas those of European nations give rights to groups. While easy to say, it is more difficult to grasp in its implications. It means, for instance, that when a European woman watches an actress in an American movie, and hears her say, *"I have my rights!"* she will probably think, *"Good for you, dear! All of us women have our rights!"* In a sense that's true; all human beings have human rights. But what the European will fail to realise is that the American has Constitutional rights only *because she is an individual*, not because she is a woman. As I said, the U.S. Constitution only gives rights to individuals. Even Companies in the States have to register as individuals!

By contrast, the Constitutions of European nations give rights to groups. In Europe, a group is much more than a gathering of individuals; it is a dynamic entity in its own right, and one whose power is greater than the sum of the powers of each member. It is this group power that is conveyed to the spokesperson for the group. In fact, a primary function of a European group is, not to encourage each individual to speak up as in the U.S., but to elect a leader who will do the speaking for them. This explains why the media only reports the opinions of the representatives of a group, not those of individuals. For all practical purpose, the opinion of the individual is of little relevance in Europe.

It is hardly surprising, then, if Americans and Europeans view the world from two essentially different perspectives. Nor is it surprising that psychologists on both sides of the Atlantic approached groups differently. As a result, Europeans developed group dynamics or processes, while their American counterparts developed group guidance and learning for individuals (thus explaining why an American psychologist like Rogers spoke so much about being a 'learner'). In other words, the different developments that appeared on either side of the Atlantic appear to have been influenced by a Constitutional bias, if not in the theorists, at least in the groups they studied.

Psychiatrists, on the other hand, tended to be individualistic in their approach to man. This was true until Dr. Murray Bowen, professor of psychiatry at Georgetown University Medical Centre, developed Family Systems Theory in the late '50s. In so doing, he belatedly introduced the concept of the group (and not just the individual) as the unit of study for the medical profession. But it is worth noting that this development only took place shortly after the end of the Korean War as I shall indicate later.

4. Conclusion

The late George Best once said that he had spent his money on alcohol, women and fast cars, and that the rest he had squandered. This led to the question, "George, where did it all go wrong?" The same question could be applied to the state of counselling today – especially in a European context. I say this because the EU requires uniformity of counsellor qualifications throughout its territory. To that end, it is putting pressure on individual governments to regulate counselling. Clearly, the time is approaching when counsellors will require either a State or EU License to function. But even now, the need for a State intervention is a sign of the confused state of counselling in the public's perception.

Part of the difficulty is that counsellors work like 'moles'; they are rarely seen at work by a public that can't tell the difference between counselling and guidance, let alone between psychotherapy and advice-giving. Like moles, they tend to work alone in a safe, underground environment that cannot be disturbed. Everyone knows they are counsellors but only their clients see the evidence. Counsellors talk and write about what they do, but rarely demonstrate their skills in a public forum; I even know some tutors of counselling who never demonstrate their skills to students in a classroom! "I am very good in a one-to-one situation, but become very shy in a group context!" How can a student learn counselling if he or she has never had a live model to follow?

All this underground secrecy surrounds counsellors with an aura of mystery that suits those who follow the paradigm of Priest. It even suits those who follow that of Wise One and who prudently keep their head down lest they be attacked. But it only splits the public in two, with some believing that counsellors can deal with everything that comes their way, while others see them as mere Agony Aunts who provide a shoulder to cry on.

Of course, psychiatrists and psychologists – indeed, most professional people in the caring industry who use 'talking therapies' – are happy to surround themselves with a blanket of (priestly) mystery as well; they seem to work from the belief that, the less the public knows about what they do, the better they will be able to function.

It was Carl Rogers who first threw open the veil that surrounded the medical Temple and made the contents available to the ordinary citizen. But then Pope John XX111 did something similar in the Catholic Church. For that, both merit our gratitude. However, as things have evolved, it has become clear that all this openness needs to be limited lest 'removing the veil' turns into a strip-tease show. There really is a difference between enabling people to take a risk - even to risk being themselves - and enabling them to turn to evil.

Once individuals turn to evil in the form of sin, sickness or crime, the social response is to fall back on the paradigm of Priest. But, equally, once societies as a whole turn away from God, not a few individuals in those societies will turn to Devils such as cults, magic and narcotics - the individualistic antithesis of the social Priest.

In the light of the above, you well might wonder, "Where did it all go wrong?" But perhaps a better question to ask might be: "Whatever happened to wisdom?" If you would like an answer to either question, read on!

2. INFLUENCE OF WAR

There is probably no better way to consider the issues of risk and evil than to focus on war. And in this chapter, I want to examine the influence that war had in bringing together European psychology and American psychiatry. Specifically, I want to look at the aftermath of the War in Korea, an era when Rogers was at his peak as a researcher in counselling. I will attempt to show a link between the end of that war and Rogers' subsequent move into encounter group work.

My reason for focusing on Rogers and encounter groups is that most counsellors use Rogerian counselling principles to some extent, and trauma work – as I hope to show later in this book – is not unlike encounter work. If so, then it makes sense to examine what happened when Rogers applied his counselling principles in a group setting. I hope to show that, while excellent in a one-to-one counselling situation, his principles and theories can be dangerous in a group, family and social setting. Futhermore, they can be quite dangerous when used by a counsellor in dealing with an adult who had been sexually abused as a child – again as I shall show later.

Having said that, I want this chapter to appear, not as a criticism of Rogers himself, but as a report on the facts as I know them of 'what happened' in California in the '60s when Rogers finally moved from his former university setting into that of the encounter culture. I believe there are many salutary lessons to be learned by counsellors who may be considering a move into trauma work.

But first, and by way of establishing a background, let's look in general terms at the association of the U.S. Army and Navy with those who deal with the human mind, namely, psychiatrists and psychologists.

1. Introduction

The U.S. Army had a tradition of using the medical profession for obvious reasons. And since psychiatry developed as a branch of medicine, it is hardly surprising that it became associated with an army which at times required treatment for a disturbed individual.

The U.S. Navy, however, had a different set of issues; unlike the army, its sailors lived and worked in confined spaces such as ships and submarines when not on leave ashore. To help it deal with groups living in enclosed spaces, the navy turned to European psychologists who specialised in Group Dynamics. Of these, Kurt Lewin was probably the most influential. Having moved from Germany to the States in the early 1930s, Lewin, a Jew and socialist, eventually became director of the Research Center for Group Dynamics at the Massachusetts Institute of Technology. He died in 1947.

It was Lewin and his associates who pioneered the idea of training groups or T-groups as they were known. The aim of the T-group was to heighten awareness of social relationships. To do this, it built on existing social skills (rather than serve as therapy as such) while dispensing with many of the conventional props and protocols of normal social interaction. As a result of Lewin's work, the National Training Laboratories (NTL) was set up by 1947 in Bethel, Maine, and funded by the Office of Naval Research.

The T-group concept gained rapid popularity within psychological circles in the States. Later, the terms, 'sensitivity training' and 'encounter groups' were coined to describe this new form of learning. The modern versions of these could be said to include conflict management, group dynamics, conflict resolution, assertiveness training for women and even encounter groups when used as a form of therapy. Together, they introduced the concept of training into education, a distinction that now permeates our own educational system; for example, you obtain a college degree in the U.K. through teaching, but an NVQ through training – just as in the U.S. you join the army for an education, but the navy for training. (The association of psychologists with the Navy explains why would-be counsellors no longer seek to be educated in the subject but, rather, to be trained in it.)

"So, what has all this to do with Rogers?" you may ask. Well, prior to World War 2, psychologists and psychiatrists worked apart as surely as did the navy and army. What eventually brought them together were military requirements arising of necessity from WW2, and brought to a head by the War in Korea ('49 – '53).

Following that war, the army's focus was on the fate of over 7000 soldiers who had been captured by the Chinese. It was concerned, not only by the mysterious deaths of so many in captivity, but also by the fact that no prisoner ever escaped from a Chinese prison camp. Indeed, no prisoner ever attempted to escape – even from one camp of 600 prisoners guarded only by 6 men with weapons! For the army, this was entirely unacceptable; if there were only 6 guards on duty, where were the other 594 who should have been supporting them? The obvious answer was - on the battlefield!

It was also inexplicable; after all, American prisoners of the Japanese during World War 2 were noted for their attempts to escape. Given such a record, it was in the army's interest to have its Colonel Meyers interview the prisoners returning from Korea in a Tokyo hospital to find out why these men were so different. The results at the time were puzzling. None had been tortured or even brainwashed if, like Rogers, you were to trust their subjective experiences. On the other hand, their behaviour indicated brainwashing, but not as the army understood the term. That was when it began to turn to psychologists and psychiatrists for an explanation.

This military need may have been behind the change in policy that led the National Institute of Mental Health (NIMH) to broaden its previous focus on psychiatric research. Instead of just looking at abnormal people in normal society, research now focused on normal people in abnormal situations (after the Vietnam war, that same focus led to the formulation of Post Traumatic Stress Disorder as we now know it).

However, 'normal people in abnormal situations' is also a fairly good description of life in a ship or submarine. And even though no sailors had been in a Korean prison camp, the U.S. navy could not but notice the similarity between a prison camp and a ship; both were confining spaces. Against this historical background, let us return to Carl Rogers in 1957, just a few years after the end of the Korean War.

2. Rogers as counsellor and researcher

Until 1957, Rogers had progressed in the expected professional style of the time, moving upwards as a psychologist. He was, of course, well known for his dedication to research. In fact, the American Psychological Association had presented Rogers, a former president of the

Association, with its first Distinguished Scientific Contribution Award in 1956. It is difficult to see how the navy in its search for the best in his profession could have overlooked such a man.

Is it then mere coincidence that, within a year of receiving his award, Rogers decided to leave the University of Chicago? Certainly it was strange; his move was viewed by all who knew him at the time as 'totally inexplicable and bewildering' according to Thorne (Carl Rogers; Sage, 1992).

Kirschenbaum, Rogers' official biographer, put it like this: "*Rogers felt sufficiently uncomfortable about the move to write a lengthy letter to the staff in an attempt to explain his decision*". Thorne, in quoting the above, adds, "*There must have been many who saw Rogers, perhaps for the first time, as a man of driving ambition who was determined to be influential even if this meant leaving his friends and disappointing those who had relied on his support*".

Given the lack of clarity as to Rogers' motives in leaving the University of Chicago, I tend to assume that he had been approached by the Navy seeking his assistance in the post Korean War era. I say this because the Navy would have been familiar with Rogers from at least two sources – the above mentioned psychological award and, secondly, because of Rogers' former book, "*Counselling with the Returned Serviceman*" that he had co-authored with J. Wallen in 1946 after World War 2.

If so, it seems to me that Rogers, a 'skilled political animal', may have sensed a golden opportunity to use the Navy's influence to enhance his own. Certainly, any possible association with the Navy would explain his feeling of being uncomfortable in his attempt to explain his decision – together with the remarkable and widespread interest in his writings after 1957, his pilgrimages of peace around the world, and his influence on presidents like Jimmy Carter (the latter involved Rogers as facilitator in brokering a peace settlement between Egypt and Israel in Camp David).

As it stands, all I can say with some degree of certainty is that around the time Rogers left the University of Chicago, he received a grant from the National Institute of Mental Health to test his theories on both 'normal' and 'abnormal' groups.

3. Rogers as trainer in groups

1957 was the year when Rogers moved from the University of Chicago, not to Yale or Harvard, but to the relatively minor University of Wisconsin, a college that is spread across four different cities. It may be coincidence, but the University's Psychology Department to which Rogers moved just happened to be in Milwaukee, a southern Wisconsin city, just across the border from Waukegan and the adjacent Great Lakes Naval Base in northern Illinois.

3.1 Rogers' work with 'abnormal' groups

Rogers' work at the University of Chicago had been mostly on intelligent but neurotic *individuals*. The University of Wisconsin gave him his first opportunity to work in its Psychiatric Unit on 'abnormal' groups (schizophrenic patients), but the 'normal' people of Wisconsin refused to participate thus eventually compelling Rogers to move to California in search of those who would. Despite this setback to his plans, it is worth noting that, in the University of Wisconsin, Rogers was given his first opportunity to work in both the departments of psychology and psychiatry, a development entirely in keeping with the adjustment of national policy in the area of mental health after the Korean War.

In 1963, Rogers ended his university career altogether, and accepted the invitation of Richard Farson, his former student, to move to La Jolla, California, initially to join the recently-formed Western Behavioural Sciences Institute (WBSI), later to establish the Center for Studies of the Person. Incidentally, La Jolla is a northern coastal suburb of San Diego; the latter just happens to be the naval base of the U.S. Pacific Fleet.

3.2 Rogers' work with 'normal' groups

So, what happened within a year of Rogers' arrival in California? Well, as Thorne puts it, "He became greatly involved in the encounter group movement, and within a year or two of arriving in La Jolla he was already seen throughout America as an elder statesman of the encounter culture".

There is, of course, an alternative interpretation of what happened in California that Thorne so delicately and tactfully skips over. As indicated above, Rogers' research had been limited to abnormal groups in Wisconsin. In order to test his theories on normal groups, Carl Rogers, a former winner of the 'Humanist of the year' award presented by the American Humanist Association, now decided - apparently with all in the Western Behavioural Sciences Institute - to make use of some two dozen catholic religious orders on the West Coast. The obvious question being: what made a humanist think that women living in convents, or men in monasteries represented normal society?

Is it possible that his selection of such subjects for research purposes may have had something to do with the fact that their life-style within a 'confined space' was not unlike that of sailors aboard ships and submarines? Were these encounters intended to benefit the participants, Rogers or some other party? Most certainly, the results would have benefited the Western Behavioural Sciences Institute, a company that not only carried out research into human relations, but also supplied training in the same for managers; common sense indicates that the latter included both naval and business.

At this point, I need to divert a little to explain the connection between navy and business; it can be summarized as follows. Big business corporations in the States take a keen interest in U.S. Naval Research on human relations; they too have people working in confined spaces (such as offices and factories). This explains the presence of human-resource managers in major companies, similar to the morale officers on a ship. It also explains why Shackleton is more relevant than Scott to American business executives; Shackleton and his team used a boat to get back to their base in the Antarctic (like the navy), whereas Scott and his team walked (like the army)! And when Rogers said (in the Gloria tapes), "Life is a risky business!" it is not unlikely that he was thinking about both naval and commercial business – and that he meant what he said!

The Western Behavioural Sciences Institute may have taken such a risk when it became involved with catholic religious groups. According to Dr. William Coulson, an associate of Rogers, "A shoestring relative of one of Rogers' Wisconsin colleagues was a member of the (Sisters of the Immaculate Heart of Mary) community", and WBSI assigned Coulson as a catholic to 'exploit the connection'. To this end, he addressed 'the California Conference of Major Superiors of Women's Religious Orders, and showed them a film of Carl Rogers doing psychotherapy'. From this it is clear that WBSI was taking advantage of personal information. And, given Rogers' prominence in this Institute, it is difficult to see how he could have remained apart from such significant if manipulative opportunism. In any case, it looks from the above that WBSI was the main driving force in identifying catholic religious groups as subjects for its research, and that the financing of this

Institute and its members came from big business.

Rogers was joined in the experiment by the above-mentioned Coulson. A graduate of Notre Dame (Ph.D. in Philosophy), the latter had been a cohort and disciple of Rogers at the University of Wisconsin, and was by then both a psychologist and a catholic who thought it possible to be a humanist at the same time. They first met in 1963, after Rogers returned to Wisconsin from his initial visit to California. When Rogers finally moved to California soon after, so did Coulson; the latter became chief-of-staff at the Western Behavioural Sciences Institute in La Jolla.

For Rogers, working in an encounter group was nothing new; he had previously experimented with the method at the University of Chicago, and could rightly be considered one of its pioneers. He now joined Coulson in their first workshop with religious groups - the Jesuits - in 1965. The latter were able to cope with the encounter groups in a university setting due to their education and training – although, subsequently, their formation programmes began to suffer after several of their novice masters introduced Rogerian principles into their training. Despite this, Rogers received two honorary doctorates from Jesuit universities.

Most other catholic groups (e.g. the Franciscans, the Mercy Sisters etc) were equally open to experimenting. On the one hand, they were open to new ideas in the wake of Vatican 2, on the other hand, they apparently were slow to read the documents of the Council, but opted instead for the 'easier approach' offered by the encounter method of training. The outcome was disastrous.

Take, for example, the IHMs (Sisters of the Immaculate Heart of Mary) in southern California. The group project with them - which began in 1966 - was terminated by Rogers, Coulson and their team of 58 other facilitators after two of the three years scheduled. By then, the IHM Sisters were ruined. As Coulson put it, "The IHMs had some 60 schools when we started. At the end, they had one. There were some 560 nuns when we began. Within a year after our first interventions, 300 of them were petitioning Rome to get out of their vows. They did not want to be under anyone's authority, except the authority of their imperial inner selves".

Coulson, of course, never disagreed with the basic principles of client-centered (non-directive, person-centered) therapy, only with their application to groups (where the issue of authority becomes more significant). In so doing, he appears to have been influenced by Abraham Maslow, the other great figure in humanistic psychology and a frequent visitor to WBSI. According to Coulson, "Maslow saw that we failed to understand the reality of evil in human life" and, "Maslow did warn us about this; Maslow believed in evil and we didn't." This in itself is surprising since all humanists believe that human nature is essentially good, creative and capable of healthy growth. However, and unlike most other personality theorists, Maslow had focused on the exceptional (healthy) - rather than on the disordered - personality. His studies had led him to see 'the reality of evil in human life'. In other words, he saw that those with humanistic and utopian views of human life - such as Rogers and Coulson - were turning a blind eye to the reality of paranoid and psychopathic personalities (among others) who were quite capable of destroying the social world for everyone else through the release of either violent or sexual desires when pursuing their 'true inner selves'! But, of course, such is the risk that is always present whenever people 'dispense with many of the conventional props and protocols of normal social interaction'.

As it was, Maslow eventually moved away from a humanism that he came to see as inadequate in explaining human life. So too did Coulson. The latter returned to his Church and wrote an article for a catholic magazine; "We corrupted a whole raft of religious orders on the West Coast in the '60s by getting the nuns and priests to talk about their distress." He even began to question the value of therapy itself in any form: "I see therapy as being fundamentally opposed to the civilized life. It's a bit like asking a competent pianist what he's doing with his fingers. In the course of the answer, the music stops because he doesn't know what he's doing with his fingers. And in order to analyse it, the music has to stop. If civilization is a kind of music, it stops when everybody gets therapy. Unfortunately, we assume now that everybody needs to get therapy". It may be for these philosophical reasons that Thorne does not view Coulson as a serious psychological critic of Rogers.

4. Chinese encounter groups

Now, you might think that the disintegration of the Sisters in encounter groups merely reflected the weakness of their religious training or system. Indeed, you might even assume that the encounter group supplied them with a 'better way'. But compare the above results with those of American POWs in Korean prison camps some 10 years previously. They, too, had been through encounter group experiences. The results? Of the prisoners involved, some 3000 died in captivity from nothing other than marasmus (i.e. progressive emaciation, especially in infants, not only through malnutrition but also through lack of human contact) or 'momism'. And none ever escaped - or even tried - since, like the Sisters, they ended up 'on their own' in the camps while 'doing their own thing'. And escape attempts - like attempts to follow your own conscience - always require cooperation with others if for no other reason than to be fully informed as to the best course of action to take.

For the Chinese, the encounter group was but one of four different techniques designed specifically to separate the prisoners from their families, country, officers and each other. The American POWs were only aware of three of these, yet entered into them voluntarily. They did so, because they 'could see no harm in it' (the 200 Turkish POWs refused to take part. All survived the prison camps). This was especially true of the encounter group sessions. In fact, therapists or facilitators were not necessarily present with the participants during the personal sharings. Each soldier was completely free to speak within the encounter group, and even within the camp. Each learned from his experience if you go by Rogers, or became an isolated individual in the prison camp if you go by the final result. In other words, what had once been a military group ended up as a gathering of lonely individuals unable to organize even a single attempt at escaping; learning from your own experience - and only from this - leads to loneliness ('the boss is always alone').

To be fair, it is important to note that Rogers did not duplicate the Chinese experiment with encounter groups, but used his own format. Still, what seems clear is that both the Chinese and Rogers implicitly encouraged participants to separate from external authority, and to pursue psychological intimacy. Both did so deliberately.

In other words, both the Chinese and Rogers encouraged participants to share in the group situation. But whereas Rogers focused on the sharing of personal experiences (rather than on the customary social relationships), the Chinese encouraged the POWs to, "Get to know each other better when here in camp" by sharing personal experiences that they had kept hidden from others.

The soldiers thought this funny but could see nothing wrong with it. However, once they opened up and began to reveal matters about themselves that were more proper to a confessional box (in the catholic tradition), they realized too late that the other troops had stopped laughing and were now listening intently. Then, when the session ended, each speaker felt the need to distance himself from the group – as surely as catholic penitents tend to distance themselves somewhat from the priest to whom they have just confessed their sins. Revealing your guilty/shameful secrets to others creates distance – as the POWs learned.

Clearly, and in a group situation, some people say too little, and others too much. Of the two, the latter is by far the more dangerous and damaging. I say this, not to stop clients from telling their hidden secrets to therapists, but to stop the latter from saying, "It is good to talk" while encouraging the former to go home and talk to their spouse (i.e. confess) prior to asking for forgiveness. No sensible person confesses his/her sins to a spouse; both have to live together and, in any case, no spouse has the power to forgive sin. Revealing your guilty/shameful secrets to inappropriate others leads to isolation, again as the POWs in Korea discovered. (Equally, such revelations can lead to one's spouse becoming traumatised - as surely as were the POWs; the latter became not only isolated but also alienated after their attachment bonds with significant others were severed over time.)

As it was, the Chinese used techniques to promote equality and intimacy among the POWs while 'dispensing with many of the conventional props and protocols of social interactions'. Those techniques had been designed to undermine the morale of the American prisoners. What is less clear is why Rogers did not know – or chose to ignore – the fact that, in the process, the Chinese had used group-work principles not unlike his own. He must have known about them, given his involvement with psychiatrists in southern Wisconsin. Most certainly, I knew of them in 1959

- but only because, as a student, I had attended a talk on that very topic, delivered by a psychiatrist, in Great Lakes Naval Base near Waukegan, northern Illinois.

5. Conclusion

Intimacy is useful in personal relationships but becomes dangerous when the issue involves group survival. When dealing with the latter, authority and control are needed, as every alcoholic, drug addict and traumatised person knows all too well. Becoming a person not only requires dealing intimately with another person, but also dealing with the issues of authority, power and control. It means trusting not only your own authority (your 'internal locus of evaluation') but also that of the other.

Rogers, of course, could never bring himself to do this – anymore than U.S. prisoners could in the Korean camps. For him, all authority outside of his own body was not to be trusted. Had he been consistent, perhaps he would have noticed that this included the authority of the client in the relationship! The client, of course, was expected to trust his own authority but, apparently, all the therapist could trust was 'the goodness of human nature'. In this way, Rogers cleverly separated authority from human nature. The former, it would seem, only existed in each individual, not in the group. Did this imply that human nature itself was only to be found in the individual, not in the group?

However, to reiterate, the Wise One had originally been a businessman. It is not surprising, then, that Rogers moved from being a researcher and teacher in the business of education, to becoming a researcher and trainer in the commercial business of WBSI (Incidentally, Rogers briefly mentioned in one encounter group which I attended, that the Navy did have an interest in his research). By moving 'up-market' in this way, Rogers showed that he truly was a wise man!

Unfortunately, it would appear that he took one risk too many when he applied his counselling theories to organised groups like religious communities; in the latter case, and like the POWs in Korea, the individuals didn't just encounter each other in the sessions, but also had to live and work with each other afterwards (in this, they differed from regular encounter groups that consisted of a variety of individuals who had come together, not only from different backgrounds but also for a relatively brief encounter, and who then dispersed later). It was mainly in the encounter groups of 'organised people in the same boat' that Rogers ran into the problem of evil, a problem which he could not accept, and one that devastated him.

As I said at the beginning of this chapter the question is not for whom did Rogers work. Rather it was whether his counselling principles were applicable in a group setting or not. I feel sure that the results of Rogers' research into human behaviour within encounter groups consisting of religious people were examined closely by both Navy and Big Business. I am equally sure that both learned a lot. It certainly explains why both shied away from the full use of Rogerian principles in either offices, ships or submarines, and why men like Gerard Egan eventually encouraged businessmen to focus more on goals - and less on the personal characteristics of a 'helper' - when managing a group.

I also hope that it cautions counsellors from dealing with the abused (like the POWs) without further training in trauma work. But more about that later in this book.

3. BEING TRUE TO YOUR INNER SELF

In the previous chapter, I showed how the Chinese separated the POWs from each other by means of encounter groups. I also indicated that they encouraged the men to separate from their officers, country and families back home. In effect, they created a climate of isolation in which they could control the POWs. Likewise, when Rogers' principles were applied to enclosed groups, they created a similar climate of isolation in which the strong were able to dominate the weak, where men could abuse women, and where women could reject their babies. And all this was carried out under the pretext of 'being true to one's inner self'.

1.1.The Centre for Feeling Therapy

At the same time that Rogers moved away from WBSI to set up his Centre for Studies of the Person in La Jolla, another group also left to set up the Centre for Feeling Therapy in Hollywood. The State of California eventually charged these men with the crime of coercing the women on 11 different occasions into aborting babies conceived in the compound, babies that the women wanted. The State Medical Board maintained that such coercive behaviour by the men was both unethical and illegal.

It appears that the argument used by the men which led the women to abort was: 'you must listen to your true inner self'. And if you are carrying a baby under your heart, or hear a baby cry, then you will become distracted from that primary commandment to listen only to your true inner self. The message given to the women was to get rid of the child either before birth through abortion, or after birth through adoption. The only person allowed to have a baby in the institution was its principal founder. All other babies were either aborted or sent away in the name of getting in touch with what Coulson termed, 'the imperial self'.

1.2 Sexual Abuse by Therapists

The same dedication to trusting only in one's own inner authority resulted in an outbreak among therapists in California at the time of having sex with their clients.

Rogers himself didn't get involved in sex games, but he couldn't prevent his followers from doing it; all he could say was, "*Well, I don't do that.*" Then his followers would say, "*Well, of course you don't do that, because you grew up in an earlier era; but we do, and it's marvellous: you have set us free to be ourselves and not carbon copies of you.*" (as quoted by Coulson)

1.3. The case of Sr. Mary Benjamin, IHM

This Sister took part in her congregation's experiment with Rogers and his team in the summer of '66. She became the victim of a lesbian seduction. Her story appeared later in a book that documented part of what happened to religious groups when exposed to Rogers' type of encounter groups.

Sr. Mary Benjamin was seduced by an older nun in her group who, experiencing the need for 'freeing herself to be more expressive of who she really was internally', told Sr. Mary Benjamin that she wanted to make love to her. Sr. Mary Benjamin cooperated but was later stricken with guilt and spoke to a priest. Unfortunately, the latter had been exposed to Rogers' theories and refused to pass judgement on her actions; he told the nun that it was up to her to decide if they were right or wrong. As a result, Sr. Mary Benjamin came to realise that she was entirely on her own – just like the POWs in Korea. In short, the liberation promised by encounter groups amounted to the experience of a terrible loneliness.

Rogers, of course, was appalled – and often depressed – by all such 'distortions', as he saw them, of his ideas. What he failed to appreciate was the influence of his own presbyterian background that had given him, unconsciously, a strict ethical foundation; he had an innate self-discipline. And as long as he was present in a group, *"Nobody fooled around!"* to quote Coulson, *"He kept people in line; he was a moral force."*

Unfortunately, most of his followers were younger people who failed to distinguish between their 'true inner self' and their libido. To them, being true to yourself meant surrendering to your instincts; for example, if you were a therapist, you tried to seduce your client and vice versa; if a married man, you seduced other women etc.. In other words, you tried to be true to yourself, not to your ethical standards, nor to your religious or married vows (the so-called 'external authorities'). The results, of course, have proved catastrophic for western civilisation in creating a generation of lonely people, many of whom later died either from alcoholism, drugs, or suicide. But, undoubtedly, all were 'being true to their inner selves' or 'following their conscience, be it right or wrong'.

2. The social problem

Any examination of the above three cases can lead to questions such as, "Were those people sinners, criminals or just plain sick?" Such questions come from those who operate from the paradigm of Priest (e.g. clergy, doctor and lawyer etc.). However, if considered from the perspective of the alternative model - that of Wise One – the same three cases give rise to an entirely different set of questions; each presents a paradox that leads to queries about the nature of culture and society itself.

A paradox is a story that goes contrary to common sense, but which in fact may be true. Indeed, it might be better to say that it is more of a story *event* than a story as such; the former makes you think about - or *experience* - the unthinkable, whereas the latter only makes you think. If so, then each of the above cases is clearly an unthinkable story event - and a paradox. Furthermore, each story defined the limits of loss as opposed to gain; the women in each case entered a relationship in pursuit of gain, but invariably experienced loss. The paradox lay in the reversal of expectation; the events were not only unthinkable but also unexpected.

The reason why nobody gave thought in advance to the unexpected is that all came from a certain culture and society where such things simply couldn't - or shouldn't - happen. In other words, the women once lived in a world of social myths and stories (like fish in water, none of us see the medium in which we live), but were compelled by later events to face reality, perhaps for the first time. The trouble was that they continued to view their former world as 'real' even as they now faced a new and different world that was equally real. In short they were confronted with two truths in conflict, the truth of a past *story* and that of a present *event*.

Now, whenever human beings are put in the position of having to choose between conflicting truths, they go into shock or become traumatised. An example of such a situation is where someone is sailing on an unsinkable ship in the Atlantic and collides with an iceberg; the shock is not so much from the event and its consequences, as from the realisation that the previous social story of unsinkability was false. If you like, traumas appear as doubles; the first is associated with the past event that sank the body, the second with the new story that sinks the mind, namely, the realisation that the social world made a fool out of the victim.

It is the wise person who knows that the social world can make fools of us all and who, when faced with our initial three cases, spends more time reflecting on a society that created a climate of evil to begin with, and less on the personal sins, crimes or sickness of individuals. As it stands, we unfortunately appear to have more Priests than Wise Ones in our modern world!

3. The counselling problem.

As indicated previously, 'following your true inner self' is too often a natural consequence of the U.S. Constitution's stance on the individual. And, indeed, the three cases in question may have been the result of cultural or social training. But it seems more than likely that they resulted from a misunderstanding of Rogers' counselling characteristics – especially *congruence* or genuineness, the opposite of phoniness.

Rogers viewed the social world and its teachings as an illusion. Consequently, he saw 'phoniness' in anyone trusting and following such an illusion. Again, this negative approach to society merely reflects that of the U.S. Constitution in giving no rights to groups. As a result, it is relatively easy to convince Americans that society is in fact an illusion.

It is, however, much more difficult to convince Europeans for whom the social world is both a way of life and of politics. All on this side of the Atlantic have an unsinkable conviction that the social world is *real*. Trying to convince Europeans that it is an illusion - and that 'all the world's a stage' - is like trying to convince the passengers on the sinking *Titanic* to board a lifeboat. Indeed, for too many Europeans, the only illusions in life are the promises of Christianity and those of European governments; in these matters, it is always easier for socialists to 'follow your true inner self'!

The truth of the matter, however, would seem to be that culture has been developed by society as a way of dealing with both the uncertain nature of life and its accompanying anxiety; all societies exist to counter the terror associated with death and change. In fact, culture could be described as 'a projection of a group's ideals that represents its shared belief in building an orderly world in the midst of chaos'. The general idea is, not to change minds, but *to reveal a basic order among things* (imitating the blue-print of stars in the sky at night) and to confirm it by forever re-presenting order in a theatrical manner. This explains the attractiveness of theatre, football matches, churches, dances and daily newspapers; all supply the consistency of order in an ever-changing environment. It is for these reasons that most knowledgeable people would agree with Shakespeare that the social world *is* an illusion, *but a necessary one* (since fantasy gives us hope).

Rogers, however, was an American for whom the social world was no more than a gathering of individuals, not an entity in its own right (a view he shared with Britain's Margaret Thatcher). Accordingly, he would not have agreed with the belief that illusion or image is necessary for the preservation of society. Nor did he believe in individuals play-acting on any social stage. Rather, he held that all this social play-acting, this 'putting on a show', was one of the major causes of so much mental illness and distress in individuals. What individuals really want is to meet *real* people, not actors hiding behind a mask or false-face.

As a result, when he called for therapists to be congruent or genuine in the counselling situation, he meant that they should be themselves in the relationship, and not be an actor, hiding behind the mask of a therapist, and play-acting the role of counsellor in front of the client-as-audience.

This stance of Rogers led some of his disciples (e.g. Carkhuff and Truax) to conclude that *the counsellor represents the opposite of the social world, but is not anti-social* – as surely as the Jester in the Royal Court (or the Joker in a deck of cards) was the opposite of the King, but not anti-royal. Likewise, to be genuine, one had to be true to oneself, and not be a phoney adopting a social role in somebody else's drama.

However, Rogers also made *empathy* one of his key characteristics. To be empathic, one has to become 'as if' the client, or to 'walk in their moccasins'. In effect, the therapist acts as if s/he was the client. This 'as if' dimension corresponds to the playing of a child in the game of 'pretend'; it requires imagination and the ability to play the part of someone other than oneself.

The capacity for 'playing the part of someone else', however, assumes that the listener can 'step out of his/her own shoes' before any transformation is possible. This means that the listener becomes *anonymous* in the relationship. While impossible for the very narcissistic, it was something that Rogers could become with remarkable ease; as Coulson put it, "*He almost vanished as a person*" when empathising.

In turn, vanishing as a person or becoming anonymous is precisely what we mean by becoming impersonal. To empathise, you first become as impersonal as Ben Kingsley had been when playing *Gandhi*. In fact, Rogers even wondered on one occasion if counsellors might not benefit from a course in theatrical acting!

We are thus faced with another Rogerian paradox in that, on the one hand, the counsellor to be genuine must *not* be an actor and, on the other hand, to be empathic has to be an actor.

Possibly to prevent a bi-polar situation from arising, Rogers gave priority to genuineness and put empathy in second place. In other words, a certain amount of 'indwelling' is called for, but what is more important is that the counsellor be able to return to her/himself at any time and not get too caught-up in the other's shoes!

Secondly, he implied that the counsellor plays the part of The Joker in the counselling situation, i.e. the figure in the deck of cards that has the ability to become any of the other cards while still maintaining its separate identity as a 'wild card'. If you like, the counsellor plays the part of The Fool (the opposite of The Wise One) who immediately puts his/her trust in a complete stranger (the new client) from the very start, and who accepts everything the other says without argument or judgement. To do so is to take a terrible risk. But, again, as Rogers put it, *"Life is a risky business"*.

It may seem like a paradox for The Wise One to play The Fool in certain situations. But then Thorne in his book noted that paradox underlined much of Rogers' thinking; it could be seen, for example, in his commitment to scientific enquiry on the one hand and, on the other hand, in his accompanying fear of the possibility that everything might one day be explicable in scientific terms. While this could be interpreted as indicating instability, it could equally be viewed as the ability to hold on to opposites so as to make life more interesting in becoming less predictable, in short, an ability to engage in creative thinking. For instance, John Keats once coined the terms, *Negative Capability*, to describe the creative act of depriving himself of personal identity in the very act of literary creation. As he wrote to his friend Benjamin Bailey on December 27th, 1817, *"Several things dovetailed in my mind, and at once it struck me what quality went to form a man of achievement, especially in literature, and which Shakespeare possessed so enormously – I mean Negative Capability, that is when a man is capable of being in uncertainties, mysteries, doubts, without any irritable searching after fact and reason..."*

Note that Keats' *Negative Capability* referred to the act of *depriving himself of personal identity* in the very act of literary creation. This 'depriving' reminds us of Coulson's comment that Rogers *'almost vanished as a person'* when empathising. It certainly resembles the teaching of Stanislavski, co-founder and co-director of the Moscow Art Theatre, when he said that an actor must be impersonal - even when the part he is playing requires that he be emotional. For example, an actor who is not impersonal when playing the part of a drunk man, will stagger around the stage, mimicking a drunk man's *behaviour*. By contrast, an actor who is impersonal will *'go into the mind'* of a drunk man, and his acting will be more restrained – since he will realise that *a drunk man is playing the part of a sober one*! It is this 'going into the mind' of another that corresponds to Rogers' 'walking in the other's moccasins' or 'indwelling'. In other words, both Stanislavski and Rogers opposed 'ham actors' who presented only *themselves* (e.g. John Wayne) while making use of *general stereotypes* to represent the other. Instead, both wanted their students to vanish as a person (e.g. Ben Kingsley) and then become 'as if' the *specific and personal character* they were studying.

Now, it is one thing to play the part of The Fool in a one-to-one situation. It is an entirely different matter to do so in a group situation. For one thing, groups have the power to *magnify* things. For example, you might smile at a comedian's jokes on T.V. when watching alone at home. But if you listened to the same comedian in a theatre, you would roar with laughter since the laughter of an audience is infectious.

Secondly, The Fool in a one-to-one situation is both human and a person. But in a social situation, where the person becomes more impersonal, so too does The Fool; the latter is magnified and moves from being the *human* Joker/Jester to becoming *the sub-human* and mischievous Imp and, eventually, the *non-human* and gleeful Demon.

To put it in another way, The Satan is anything but human and personal; rather, he is both inhuman and impersonal. That's why we use the term 'evil' when speaking about a person who has *transgressed* or *gone beyond the limits* of the personal i.e. was impersonal when doing 'bad' things, or who treated another as if they were not there as a person, but only as a thing or a nobody. And while moral theologians might view evil as *'anything that diminishes the possibility of good'*, psychologists tend to view evil as *'anything that increases the possibility of harm'*. In either case, the 'anything' includes *more than behaviour*; it could, for example, include tsunamis, pollution, a nation's economic system, famine, war, racism, sexism, religious discrimination, etc.

However, Rogers, being American, did not believe in a group entity. Nor did he have any time for the impersonal behaviour exhibited by people in group situations. Nor had he any awareness, it seems, of how impersonal he became when empathising (his disciples will argue that he became entirely *personal* at such times. I don't disagree. I merely suggest that he was both personal and impersonal i.e. *was a creative person*, capable of balancing opposites, but unable to see the impersonal aspects of his own behaviour). Furthermore, he had given up believing in an impersonal God. Accordingly, since he now rejected the impersonal in any shape or form - religious, secular or social - it follows that he did not believe that there was such a thing as evil to begin with. Rather, he maintained that individual humans were *fundamentally good at heart* and could grow of their own accord (like a potato) if surrounded by the right 'climate'.

It was this naive illusion that led Rogers to put *congruence* (being true to your inner self) before *empathy* in his hierarchy of values. But it is worth noting that at least he *linked* them in the counselling situation. However, when he moved into the encounter group situation, he appears to have *assumed* that all present would speak from a position of genuineness, and would listen empathically to what others said. Whether they did so or not is debatable.

My limited experience of his encounter-group sessions led me to conclude that people were genuine when speaking, but supplied little outward evidence of empathy when listening. In short, genuineness and empathy became separated, with congruence and its narcissistic individualism coming to the fore, while the more socially oriented empathy took a back seat.

It also seems that, in wider society, Rogers' concept of *'being true to your own inner self'* became better known than his gallant efforts to develop a world of empathic listeners, of people who would enter the world of another through *indwelling* and through their *commitment* to unconditional love. If so, and in the card-game of life, it seems true to say that the King will inevitably replace the Joker and, in a group context, the 'imperial self' will invariably replace the 'acting or serving self'.

4. Conclusion

One significant point to note is Rogers' decision to put congruence or genuineness before empathy; clearly, his intention was to encourage student counsellors to be themselves in the relationship. There is, however, another possible explanation, namely, that he as an American put emphasis on the *individual*. And there is little doubt that being 'true to your inner self' is very individualistic in orientation; the three cases referred to at the start of this chapter illustrate that point.

By contrast, empathy is a *social* and developmental phenomenon. Children learn about empathy by playing games of 'pretend' with other children. Even adults require an 'other' in order to empathise (although some will argue that it is possible to empathise with yourself. To this I can only respond, "Yes, and you can also have sex with yourself as well!" To me, 'playing with yourself' is indicative of a narcissistic mentality, and loneliness is not necessarily a state that fosters healthy development). Empathy - like mature sex - is a form of communication; it is a way of *being* with another. It is not something you *do* - either to or for another. This explains why the very narcissistic cannot empathise.

I think it unfortunate that Rogers decided to put congruence first. Like the cowboy in the movie *High Noon*, he kissed his girlfriend *Empathy* goodbye, and rode off into the sunset on his horse *Congruence*. It is also unfortunate that his equally macho followers tried to imitate him, but had the re-occurring habit of falling from their high horses as we have seen. Most certainly, had counselling been first developed in Europe, it would have resulted in a reversal of those priorities; empathy would have preceded genuineness in importance.

What reinforces this belief is that all the counselling problems that later emerged in the States centred on genuineness, not empathy. For one thing, clients will forgive your inability to empathise correctly, but will be less forgiving if you are morally incorrect when being 'true to your inner self'.

But, perhaps, the greatest problem of all was that Rogers and his followers succeeded in diverting everybody's attention away from wisdom and towards the personal characteristics of a helper. Instead of encouraging people to be wise when dealing with others, he wanted them to become, not what they actually were, but what he believed them to be - 'good' people. It was his humanistic belief in human goodness that blinded him to the reality of fallen human nature, and which made him believe that there was no such thing as evil. It was his former religious beliefs that made him a moral force in encounter groups, not his humanistic philosophy or his counselling talents. And it was his lack of belief in the *social* that blinded him to his own impersonal behaviour when empathising.

I think it true to say, however, that Rogers, the researcher in counselling, the learner in the classroom and the leader in the encounter group, invariably worked from the paradigm of Wise One, not that of Priest. As a wise man he was prepared to take risks in pursuit of a goal. But when those risks led to evil, he had no alternative paradigm to fall back upon; after all, he did not believe in God, let alone priests! Possibly because of this intransigent stance, he could only become depressed when confronted with the evils of this world.

Still, he left behind something for us to learn, namely, that when dealing with the *personal* i.e. intimacy and its risks, you might find it useful to operate from the paradigm of Wise One. But when dealing with the *impersonal* i.e. authority and evil, you will find it very useful indeed to have the paradigm of Priest to fall back upon.

4. THE IMPERSONAL

Earlier in the book, I presented an aspect of Carl Rogers' work that rarely appears in this country, namely his association with business, naval and commercial. The link may be somewhat tenuous in this presentation, but I believe that his connection with the Western Behavioural Sciences Institute is a strong indication that he really was 'a skilled political animal' as Thorne put it. This will be fairly shocking on this side of the Atlantic - especially to many counsellors who hold Rogers in esteem, and who are particularly attracted to his counselling theories about *intimacy*. But as already noted, Rogers came to the fore, not only in the aftermath of the war in Korea, but also in the wake of two previous world wars. By that stage, everyone was weary with the inhumanity of warring *authorities*, and hungered for a little human *intimacy*. Everyone was vulnerable.

They were also beginning to doubt the validity of authority itself. As a result, when Rogers began to preach the Gospel of Doubt, he found a large congregation eager to receive his message: *do not trust authority but doubt everything they say*. This doctrine explains why Rogers' favourite saint was Doubting Thomas. It may also explain why, in the previous chapter, I went out of my way to describe his views on *empathy*; there is a clear relationship between his 'indwelling', 'going into the world of another', 'seeing the world through the other's eyes', 'getting into his skin (moccasins rather than shoes)' on the one hand and, on the other, St Thomas' remark, *"Until I have seen in his hands the print of the nails, and put my finger in the mark of the nails and my hand in his side, I will not believe."* In fact, Rogers had once given serious thought to becoming a minister in his own church; he had even attended a liberal school of theology where he and others soon reasoned their way out of religion (as surely as the Sisters later reasoned their way out of Religious Life with Rogers' help). No longer believing in God, Rogers began to believe in 'the goodness' of humanity. He turned initially to individual counselling, and later to encounter groups (or congregations) in the hope of finding that missing and spiritual 'goodness' or 'presence' (i.e. the mother whom he as a child had never been able to influence) in psychology; individuals always search for what they never had.

It is of interest to note that Gerard Egan, the other leading figure in the world of counselling, was also associated with big business; his specialty was Organisational Development. But whereas Rogers' characteristics of a helpful person had previously been introduced to the world of business in places like the Western Behavioural Sciences Institute, Egan later reversed this process; he applied the principles of business management to the counselling world while holding on to Rogers' core characteristics to a certain degree; his developmental model of counselling included management principles not to be found in Rogers' work. Furthermore, Egan had designed his model to be a short-term counselling (or management) package covering a four to ten week period at the most (this brevity made it the most popular in the world - or wherever administrators required a 'quick

turn-over' of clients to make their reports look good).
It should be noted, however, that the Egan model is only
useful in situations where clients have to manage *problems
that are theirs*. It was not designed for the management of
disasters; in the latter instance, *the problems are created by
someone - or something - else*. In other words, Egan's
developmental approach is useful in bringing out the best in
people who have to work, say, as a team in an office. It is
not particularly relevant in situations where a terrorist
bomb – or an 'Act of God' - has destroyed the office. In such
cases, an *insurance* agent is required, not an organisational
development person. And in the field of counselling, such
'insurance agents' are known today as *trauma counsellors*.
In ancient times, however, they were known as *priests*.

1. Insurance agents.
Primitive tribes and traumatised people have
something in common; both have experienced the terror of
a child when facing the unknown. In fact, terror is the
predominant feeling associated with religion throughout
the world. It was the feeling that first drew humans to
form groups, tribes and society for survival purposes, and
then to look up to Higher Powers (as small children look up
at their parents) for help; the social world and archaic
religions were born together – not unlike Siamese twins.
To settle themselves in a terrifying environment,
primitive people built settlements. Subsequent generations
learned to repeat their archetypal building patterns. And
since the central model for the construction of all other
buildings in the settlement was The Temple, the priest
functioned as architect for society in building 'a better
world'. The blue-print he used was the sky - especially at
night - since it revealed an arrangement of heavenly bodies
that remained fairly constant, and could serve as a model
to be followed when laying out settlements (hence the

arrangement of archaic structures such as the pyramids in Egypt, Stonehenge in England, and the Newgrange mounds in Ireland). Such patterns introduced the theme of order into human awareness, and eventually led to The Priest becoming the paradigm for all who opposed disorder in the form of sin, crime and sickness. In short, the priest was both architect for society, and insurance agent who protected it from any return of the terror.

2. The protector

Someone has pointed out that there are no atheists on a battlefield; all soldiers turn to God for protection before battle. However, after the battle, all traumatised soldiers invariably cry out for their mothers; the need *for protection* is replaced by the need *for soothing* once the emergency passes.

The interesting point to notice is the movement from 'him' to 'her'. All will acknowledge that the latter movement to 'her' for soothing is entirely instinctive, but few seem to be aware that the former movement to 'him' for protection is equally instinctive. Clearly, both movements are taken from the model of the human family where the father protects and the mother soothes. These facts are based, not on cultural or social conditioning, but on the obvious need of children for their mothers. Men and women may be prepared to lay down their lives for their children, but both are trapped by what has been called, 'The tyranny of the minority' or what I call 'The need of the child'. This need or tyranny demands that the woman must live for the sake of the child. As a result, both parents accept that, in an emergency situation, the first to die for the protection of the family will be the father. This is the 'natural way'; any reversal of roles, say, where the mother goes out to defend her husband and children, is against 'the laws of nature' as determined by a child. When it comes to the survival of children, adults simply can't afford to follow *the laws of your true inner self* as we saw in the previous chapter.

It was this understanding of father as protector in the family that led humanity to view the Deity-who-protects in masculine terms as God the Father. It also led to the priest becoming, not just a spiritual insurance agent, but also a moral protector of society. This combination of masculine terms - Deity, father, priest and protector - led eventually to our understanding of the *impersonal*.

3. The impersonal

The terms *personal* and *impersonal* had their roots in ancient Greek and Roman theatre. There an actor wore a mask to represent the character he was playing on the stage. The hidden actor who spoke was the person (in Latin, *per sonare*, 'to speak through'), and the mask through which he spoke was an impersonal face (or *persona*) that never changed no matter who the actor was. It was this impersonal face that became so fascinating - and so useful - to the social world.

3.1 The mask also served a useful purpose in creating *mystery*; nobody knew for sure the identity of the actor. And mystery to the child-like is always magical (which is why magicians are so popular). The impersonal lends itself to mystery, magic and, eventually, to religion. Incidentally, our impersonal term *Mister* was derived from *mystery* and is exclusively applied to men. And since religion also deals with mystery, then only Misters could become priests! Remove both the *Mister* and the impersonal from the priesthood and, to that extent, you remove the mystery from religion; instead of a spiritual entity, the result will be viewed, most likely, as a social club for the pious.

In other words, evil primarily refers to *things* that could cause harm (such as 'the evil eye' etc), and it originally was the function of the Priest to deal with both holy and unholy things. By contrast, the Wise One dealt with *persons* who took chances with such things. This means that the Priest who opposes evil deals with *things*, while the Wise One who opposes risks deals with *persons*. The distinction between a 'thing' and a 'person' is fundamental to understanding the nature of the impersonal, the priesthood – and of evil itself.

A 'thing' originally was a **group meeting or assembly** - as in the Latin, *Res Publica* or Republic, 'the public thing' - but its meaning evolved over time so that it now refers to any *impersonal* item. However, *"Doing your own thing"* still implies running your own group independently of the official group! And when a man says, "I have a thing going for her", he probably intends an impersonal *meeting* in the hope of a future and personal relationship. In all instances, the 'thing' is entirely *impersonal*.

Given the association of a 'thing' with a group, and a 'mask' with an actor, it follows that the traditional role of Priest involved his wearing the mask of holiness when dealing with the 'things' of God, and when protecting the community from those 'things' that symbolised evil. That was why only a male could be a priest; men dealt with 'things' (while women dealt with 'persons'). And on the religious stage, only men served as priests to remind other men that they *as men* represented the Deity who protects all – and to behave themselves accordingly!

3.2 The impersonal is also useful in the creation of myths. The latter are stories created by society to make sense of its history; they address the question of *change* in the social world, changes brought about by death in its many forms. For while stability required that nothing should change, it was a simple matter of observation that nothing was permanent. Social myths showed how a group could change and still remain constant. They did this by establishing a pattern of story in three parts. First, the world was once wonderful. Second, a conflict of opposites threatened the harmony of the group. Third, a godlike figure intervened to restore peace and reconciliation, but usually died in the process.

An example of a social myth was the latest film of *'The Titanic'*. To begin with, the different classes occupied their own sections in the ship, illustrating how 'wonderful' their world was! Secondly, a conflict arose between Rose and her fiancé that threatened to destroy the equilibrium of that society. Thirdly, Jack – the godlike figure – appeared to save the day, but died in the process. The point to notice is that each character and fixture in the play *symbolised* something beyond itself. For example, the ship (which Rose described as a 'slave ship') symbolised technological society, and the human figures symbolised the social classes of Europe from which all were moving on their journey to the New World. The fact that each character symbolised something beyond himself or herself meant that the characters were entirely impersonal. What was important was not who they were, but *what they symbolised.*

Social myths were shaped to help society remember the meaningful. If you like, *myth, memory and meaning* are almost interchangeable terms; myths are memorable, memories are meaningful and meanings are mythical. That's because all are based on the themes of *community and continuity* that are so vital for the maintenance of society in a forever-changing world.

It is unfortunate that modern people have lost their understanding of myth and of the illusory nature of the social world. At least, since Shakespeare's time, most have viewed the social world as a stage on which each actor was expected to perform in a manner that made it simple for others to identify him or her; for example, the doctor dressed in white, the cleric dressed in black etc; each dressed in the suit that suited! In other words, the outer show that we put on is all the public sees; this is our persona. By contrast, nobody can see the inner soul (self or person) behind the show.

3.3 The interesting point to note in the show is that the hidden actor must always perform as did those who went before him; *"Things have to be done the way we always did them!"* This implies that each actor must set an example for the next generation; if the performer's behaviour was not exemplary, his actions would be meaningless. For instance, if an actor, playing the part of the mythical Hamlet, came out on the stage wearing blue jeans while strumming a guitar, his performance would certainly not be memorable for the simple reason that the spectators would find it meaningless. Likewise if a businessman went to work without his grey suit, but dressed instead in casual clothes, his clients would have reason for not doing business with him. It is this formal, ritualistic and exemplary behaviour that is both expected by society, and necessary for its survival. Everything in the social world has to be carried out in an *impersonal* manner. In a changing environment, everyone hungers for consistency and continuity.

3.4 As mentioned before, it was all this impersonal acting on social stages that Rogers - and most young people - viewed as 'phoney'. Being an idealist, he thought it possible to create a world of persons who would just be themselves. In effect, he wanted actors to move onto a stage with no make-up or appropriate clothing when playing the part of someone else, and he wanted people in the social world to do something similar. But, the whole point of both theatre and social world is that everyone is called upon to act-out the part of an identifiable other. For example, if John Brown is employed to teach in a secondary school, he plays the part of 'teacher' once he enters the school; *he is not employed to be himself*, but to be what the principal wants him to be – another version of the principal, someone who will uphold the school's standards and live up to its expectations.

Counselling, as Rogers intended, was meant to be the only form of work where the *person without a mask* was both necessary and acceptable. The 'person' (or actor) corresponded to the mother in the family from a child's point of view. The 'mask' was analogous to the father, the impersonal one who protected her and was always outside working! And the paradigm of Wise One was consistent with both.

There is, of course, a time to wear a mask, and a time to let down your guard. But, when danger's around, the wise put on their helmets in a hurry! Likewise, when clients have been exposed to evil, wise counsellors change their paradigm to that of Priest. As I hope to show, counsellors of necessity must become as *impersonal* as The Priest when confronted by evil.

4. The question of evil

It has taken the issue of trauma to re-awaken many of us to the idea of God. The psychiatrist, Judith Lewis Herman, noted in her book, *Trauma and Recovery*, that only the language of religion described the experience of the abused; at least all who had been through the experience summarized it by saying, *"I have been through hell!"* that is to say, they used a religious term with which psychiatrists do not usually feel comfortable. She also went on to note that, at the time, all models of recovery from trauma were based on the AA programme; they involved turning to a Higher Power.

To understand this experience of 'going through hell' or of experiencing evil, consider the case of a mother in a room with her infant. Should she leave the room, she vanishes from the child's sight and, as a result, the latter has his first experience of what we mean by evil, namely, *"There's nothing there!"* It is this experience of nothingness - or of an absence - which terrifies and that describes evil – the *'absence of the good'*. If you like, evil is not unlike the colour black (which is actually the absence of colour) or of the number zero (which is the absence of a number); it refers to the *absence* of something or of someone. And it is this sense of an absence that fills people with dread. Accordingly, when someone has been sexually abused, they sense that they had been treated as a 'nothing' by another human being – as if they had not really been there as a person. In short, they had been treated as if *an impersonal thing*.

To some extent, this explains the limitation of counselling along Rogerian lines. The approach of Carl Rogers - or, for that matter, Gerard Egan - is effective when dealing on a one-to-one basis with a client on matters concerning *personal* relationships. Both approaches, however, are ineffective when it comes to *social* problems like sexual abuse, that is to say, where the client has been exposed to evil through the *impersonal* behaviour of another (by a social problem I mean one that the client cannot 'own' since the 'owner' is someone in the social world). In such cases, the client is called upon by the therapist *to separate* from the other's problem, and to exercise control and authority; the client should not go into the problem and talk about it, or become intimate with it - as called for in the theories of Rogers and Egan. Indeed these latter approaches can harm the person by unwittingly reinforcing his/her attachment to the abuser.

When the question is one of *evil* or when the 'badness' is *impersonal*, therapists need to take seriously the principle that, *'Evil attaches'*; like a Black Hole in space, it fascinates even as it draws us to our doom should we get too close. An example of this morbid and addictive fascination appeared after the collapse of the twin towers in New York; children tended to replay the videos of the event continuously. In a similar manner, abusive behaviour by others both fascinates by its horror, and draws the abused unwittingly into an obsession; they go through life forever denouncing immorality with little awareness that, the more they do so, the more they are becoming *addicted to morality*. If so, and in such cases, the principle of intimacy has to be replaced by that of authority and control; nobody can overcome evil by going into it or by trying to understand it, only by turning to the opposite – *separating* from it, i.e. imitating the God who is separate (holy); "*Get behind me, Satan!*" If you like, and in similar cases involving evil, therapists adopt an approach not unlike that of exorcists.

Let me give you an example of the use of this principle of separation in counselling. A young, adult female who had been abused as a child came to me since she felt the need to talk about it to someone but couldn't due to shame, embarrassment etc. While she could tell me in a very general manner that she had been sexually abused, she simply was unable to spell this out in more specific terms, a matter that she was determined to face. I used Rogers' counselling principles with her to make her feel safe and to gain her trust. When, after a few years of therapy (in which she spoke mostly about her current life), she reached the point of deciding to tell me exactly what had happened to her in the distant past, and I sensed that, this time, she was indeed going to do so, I broke in to say, "*Hold it! I don't need to know the details. Perhaps the police or social workers need to know, but I don't. If what happened shocked you, it will probably shock me! What is important is, not that you tell me but, that you now have the courage to tell those who need to know.*" Her entire body sank back in the chair with obvious relief. (As with similar case histories in this book, details have been changed to make identification impossible).

By contrast, I have become aware that too many counsellors actually encourage their clients to become more specific (concrete) in spelling out the intimate details of sexual abuse (and even the *name* of the abuser!), apparently on the false assumption that, "It is good to talk!" They have little awareness that such activity can result in the traumatised client *reliving* the experience (and in the counsellor having a legal obligation to report the crime) whereas ordinary clients merely *recall* their experiences. If so, it is hardly surprising if such a client becomes re-traumatised.

5. Dealing with evil

To avoid causing harm, it is imperative that the counsellor who has brought the client to the rim or lip of the volcano, breaks in to encourage them to *step back* from the lava, not to 'go into it' or, worse still, to enter it accompanied by a therapist with little understanding of the nature of hell! If anything, the therapist has to model *wise* behaviour, and the latter requires the ability to recognize danger and to know when to step back from it. This is what the client (who is now *blind to danger* due to trauma) has to learn – how to put distance between themselves and evil *by imitating the therapist's behaviour.* In short, *the therapist models what the client has to do.*

Modelling wise behaviour is enhanced when you focus on the well-being of the client, and not on the details of the abuser's behaviour; it suffices to have the latter described in the most general terms possible, e.g. *"So what we are talking about is sexual abuse in some form?"* That form may even include terms such as 'rape', 'oral sex' etc but, even then, such terms should be used cautiously by you – especially when the client tries to avoid them. And most certainly, go no further in exploring the details. To do so would be *to focus on morality* (i.e. actions or doing) whereas what you focus on is *the person* of the client (her being) and on her *dignity/worth*. (The difference between a 'person' and an 'individual' is that the former term invariably implies *dignity*, whereas the latter merely implies a unit - human or otherwise - with no reference to social value.)

As for treatment, nobody in their right mind would deal with an alcoholic by offering him a drink, and nobody would treat an abused person by encouraging him/her to sip from a chalice already poisoned by abuse, i.e. *"Let's go into your experience and talk about it"*. The only known way to break this *addiction* to morality is to focus on its opposite i.e. on *devotion* to a Higher Power/God. It is to focus on 'being' and not 'doing'. It is to introduce the idea of the impersonal or of the transcendent (the holy) as advocated by religion.

Such a stance, of course, creates problems for a therapist with no religious background. In such instances it suffices to adopt the solution created by Alcoholics Anonymous; speak about a 'Higher Power', i.e. use terms that do not exclude God but which can also include one's society or group. What is important is not what term you use ('God', 'A Higher Power' or 'The social world') but that you introduce the idea of *the impersonal* into a client's thinking. It is this impersonal dimension that is required to distract the abused, the addicted and the obsessed away from their over-attachment to personal morality and to its heroes and villains. By becoming more impersonal and anonymous (as in AA, or as Rogers was with a client), the client is able to put distance between themselves and 'what happened'.

6. Conclusion

It may be noticed that I have linked the father with *impersonal authority*, and the mother (and family) with *personal intimacy*. I do so because this is how a child sees the world. If you need proof, consider the stories that children love – fairytales. In these, men can be turned magically into animal forms, but women can't. A Prince can be changed into a frog, a bad boy into a donkey, a violent male into a beast, indeed, a young girl can even be a half-fish (mermaid), but *a grown woman must always keep a human form* – even when she is 'wicked' (step-mother or witch). As I said, it would be too terrifying for a child to think of his or her mother as 'absent' or as anything other than human, personal and close.

What the terms *impersonal* and *personal* have in common, however, is that both refer to the *connection* you have with others. If the connection is based on the issue of power, then the two parties hold a formal, impersonal and serious *meeting*. But if it is based on that of love, then the two parties enter an informal, personal and playful *relationship*. Any failure to distinguish between power (the instincts of sex and anger) and love (free will and choice) can result in a failure to distinguish between a *meeting* and a *relationship*; the former involves an association of roles, the latter an association of persons.

This may seem like academic semantics but is fundamental to understanding "*Where did it all go wrong?*" when people come together. It certainly explains what can go wrong when he, for example, approaches her intending a meeting, and she assumes that he intends a relationship. In such instances, he really is from Mars, and she is definitely from Venus!

Precisely the same dynamics appear in the connection between adult sex abuser and child 'victim'. The predator - usually in disguise - approaches his target in search of a meeting, while the child views it as a (flattering) relationship. It is hardly surprising, then, if the once-bitten child shies away from all future relationships!

Part of your job is to show the adult survivor of child

sexual abuse that the original 'happening' was, in fact, a meeting and not a relationship. As such, it has to be viewed in a very cold, clinical and impersonal manner, not in emotional terms (angry, hurt, guilty, ashamed, depressed, devastated etc) when referring to it in the future. I shall show how this is done in a later chapter.

5. TRAUMA WORK

Time, they say, destroys innocence. It certainly did in the case of child sex abuse. The latter words have been used with such consistency by the media that they now have taken on a life of their own. Everyone from priests to doctors to police speaks about child sex abuse; in this, all share a common vocabulary centring on the term *abuse*.

Frankly, I'm not too happy with our use of the latter term. After all, those who suffered have to deal with the traumatic consequences of a predator's aggression against them, an aggression that happened to express itself in a sexual form, and an aggression that effectively put a child's nervous system into serious shock. In saying this, I make no apology for the threefold use of the term *aggression*. I am from the North of Ireland where, if a letter contained a bomb, we called it a 'letter-bomb', not 'letter-abuse'; it was the content that mattered, not the form in which it appeared.

Likewise, to talk about 'sexual abuse' is to focus on the form, not the content – *aggression*. If it looks like a wolf, walks like a wolf, talks like a wolf, eats lambs like a wolf (while dressed like a sheep), it is probably a wolf. So why accuse it of being a lamb abuser? Why not call it what it is - a hungry wolf? Why speak about 'child sexual abuse' (a phrase which subtly implies that the child sexually abused somebody else) when *'the hunting of children for sexual purposes'* more accurately describes the activity? It was hunting that destroyed innocence, not just time.

Could it be that we have adopted the language of our American friends who find it more useful in courtrooms to speak about 'abusive' behaviour than 'aggressive' behaviour (the term *abusive* refers to the *illegality* of an action, whereas *aggressive* does not; the latter can even be an admirable characteristic in the States – as is *hunting* in Europe)? Likewise, it was American lawyers and their medical advisors who first used the term *disorder* (as in Post Traumatic Stress Disorder) for litigation purposes; in U.S. courts, you can't get compensation for 'being the way you are', but you can if you call the latter condition a 'disorder'! The point to notice is how easily American legal jargon can become the norm for English-speaking countries elsewhere on the planet.

Something similar happened to the word *shock*. Originally an agricultural term referring to sheaves of grain stacked as a 'shook' or 'stook', it was later applied to the forceful collision of armies in battle (as their spears were forced upwards by the collision, and created a scene not unlike that at harvest time). The medical profession next used it to describe the consequences of battle wounds, and said that the trauma or breaking of bones had been due to the shock of a blow or collision. Finally, they applied the term *trauma* to psychological shock and, of course, ended up subsequently in courtrooms speaking about a 'disorder'. What started on a farm, ended up in court!

In any case, abuse (I resign myself to using the term) and shock are now associated with trauma for most of us. That shock can be due to man-made causes (e.g. car crashes, the sinking of ships etc) or from natural disasters (like tsunamis, earthquakes etc). However, for the purposes of this book, it primarily refers to the after-affects of abuse. And the first thing you need to know is that *all abuse is traumatic in its effects*.

Every sensible person will agree that physical, sexual and emotional abuse - even neglect - of children is shocking, meaning that it is shocking to those who hear about it. Most will probably assume that the child was also shocked by the abuse at the time. To a large extent this is true – in the sense that *the body* of the child was traumatised by the event. It is, however, questionable whether the *mind* of the child was also traumatised. I say this because the human mind has a unique ability to protect itself from dangerous thoughts; the limbic system seems to prevent another part of the brain from even *thinking* such thoughts. If so, it is true to say that the child at the time probably had '*no idea*' as to what was happening. On the other hand, it is also true to say that the child can dissociate, with one part (the *body*) living in a constant state of terror, while the other part (the *mind*) goes on merrily with life as if nothing had happened.

It is often much later - when the person 'learns the truth' about the event - that he or she is confronted with a conflict between two truths (as mentioned earlier in the book) and can then become *consciously* shocked.

The implication in this for you as a counsellor is that you can be approached by abused clients at different stages in their 'learning the truth'. Some don't know they were abused, but come because they feel depressed; they don't see any link between their current feelings and a distant event that is only recalled as fleeting memories – if at all! Others come because they feel depressed, know they were abused in the past but don't connect the past event with their present feeling. Still others arrive feeling depressed, knowing of their past abuse, associating both feeling and event in a vague way, but know nothing about trauma and its effects; in this scenario, they truly believe that their problems centre on sex abuse!

The truth of the matter, however, is that all such clients - at whatever stage they may be in - are dealing with trauma in the present, not sex abuse in the past. They have to learn how to deal with current traumatic *symptoms* of their own, not with former illegal/immoral/diseased *problems* of someone else.

If so, it follows that you have to learn about such symptoms. If you don't, you could end up in a situation not unlike a Health Farm where a heavy lady comes in to lose weight; if neither she nor the fitness expert knows anything about pregnancy, then both could be in trouble. Likewise in counselling where a client arrives weighed down by depression and anxiety; if neither you nor your client know a thing about trauma and its symptoms, you both may end up in trouble!

1. Psychiatry

It is beyond the scope of this book to go into the medical symptoms in detail; if interested, read my former book, *'The Sky Before the Storm'* that was written for those injured by the 'troubles' in Northern Ireland, and which is only available there (see bibliograpy for further information). I shall limit myself to some general remarks based on *'The Future of Trauma Work'* as it appeared in *The Journal of Counselling and Psychotherapy, May 2004, Vol 15, No. 1*. In this article, Clare Pointon recorded her interview with the respected trauma expert, Bessel van der Kolk, Professor of Psychiatry and Director of the Trauma Centre in Boston.

1.1. Introduction

Van der Kolk's theories have become increasingly focused on how trauma affects the body rather than just the mind. He notes that the imprint of trauma is primarily on the five senses of the body, and that it takes work on these

- rather than talking – to facilitate their disappearance over time.

At the core of his theory is the issue of how people calm themselves down. In infancy, the mother does this for the child through touch, rocking, facial expressions, and sound. Later the growing child learns how to calm itself when dealing with the surrounding environment.

However, when a person experiences trauma, they become highly aroused and, for a time, lose this capacity to calm themselves. But if at such moments they are able to respond to those around them, they will be able to think clearly, and are likely to cope fairly well. It is those who cannot do this who remain in a state of high bodily arousal, unable to calm themselves nor use their environment to do so, who end up, *"Taking leave of their senses"*, organising their inner world around the trauma, and often going on to develop Post Traumatic Stress Disorder.

1.2. Results of research using brain scans on volunteers as they recall their traumas:
1. The right hemisphere of the brain (associated with *emotional states and autonomic arousal*) is lit up.
2. Parts of the frontal lobe (that deal with the capacity *to plan, rationalise, inhibit inappropriate behaviour*) are shut down.
3. The limbic system (that part which interprets what is *safe or dangerous* in the world) and the brain stem (that governs *sleeping, breathing, urinating and chemical balances*) are most affected by trauma.
4. The amygdala (part of the limbic system that *organizes movement in the body*) acts as a kind of 'smoke detector', sending out alarm signals when the person enters a situation that might remind her of the original trauma. The more immobile the person was during the original event, the more at

risk of trauma and the more active the 'smoke detector'.

In short, when recalling their traumas, people have trouble **thinking** and **speaking** clearly and precisely about what is going on *at the present moment*. Nor can they **imagine** how things could change (trauma affects the prefrontal cortex of the brain).

It is of interest to note that **movement** (fight or flight) during the original traumatic event reduces the risk of the person becoming traumatised. This same theme of *movement* may be noticed in the following section.

1. 3. Significance for treatment

Once you realise that you are dealing with a traumatised person, begin by teaching them how 'to ground' themselves i.e. to keep both feet on the floor and experience their seeing, hearing, smelling, tasting, touching (e.g. the texture of the chair); in short, *teach them how to feel safe in their body* or *become firmly anchored in the present*. Focus on their *five senses* - not on their feelings - so that they can become *grounded* before they move.

Van der Kolk favours their using yoga or T'ai chi to this end. The idea is to help them *to stay in their bodies and be still'*. *"It is our bodies more than our minds that control how we respond to trauma"*. In short, any exercise that uses *movement* (dance, karate etc) to empower is useful.

He also is a great believer in Eye Movement Desensitisation Reprocessing (EMDR), an approach used to help clients deal with their traumas; he *'guides patients through specific eye movements at key moments, while thinking about a traumatic experience'*. *"Eye movements seem to set up a state of body-mind de-arousal, which makes it possible for the mind brain to integrate the fragments of the traumatic memory that cannot be integrated when the organism is in a state of high arousal"*.

All the above are required since, *"Talking may help* (the client to) *override the body's responses to traumatic triggers but it won't get rid of them"*. His advice to counsellors working with trauma is: *"Go easy on the narrative"*, and not to nudge the client into it with, *'tell me more'*. Of course, counsellors without training in EMDR should not engage in this form of treatment.

In one-to-one work, the counsellor may have to use his/her *imagination* to visualise the future for a traumatised client; *"I notice you have a great command of English. Have you ever given any thought to writing a book?"* In other words, you may have to use *your* imagination since your client's has been damaged by trauma.

In group work, and after the speaker tells his/her story, it helps for the group to *create a new outcome, a different ending to the story*. This is because, with a damaged imagination, the client cannot do this alone. One way to do it is to ask the group to respond to an individual's negative story by *designing a positive image* when constructing a collage as a summary of what they heard.

1.4. Conclusion

"I believe the most important thing that all mental health professionals need to know is not how to interpret complex behaviour, but how to help people to stay on an even keel", according to Van der Kolk. *"If someone is on an even keel, they are in a physiological condition where they can keep hold of their senses. This means that they can continue to be able to think and be quiet."*

Of course, staying on an even keel is even more important for a counsellor who wants to become involved with trauma work. To that end, I would now like to show you a model of trauma work or a process with which clients seem comfortable when talking about themselves.

2. Psychology

While the above material puts emphasis on the *body* as it affects the human mind, the following will focus more on how the *group* affects it. This is the work of psychologists. And, as you may recall from chapter 1 of this book, it was European psychologists who first developed theories about group dynamics.

You may also have noticed how the previous psychiatric material focussed on *movement* of the body. It should not be surprising, then, if the psychological approach also centres around movement and, for our purposes, the movement that occurs in the process of therapy itself.

The movement in counselling for someone who uses Carl Rogers' approach is fairly straightforward; you simply follow the client! By contrast, the process for Egan was a series of stages that served more as a rough map or guide than as a blue print to be followed precisely. Many counsellors like myself tend to visualise the process as a 'diving operation', involving a descent by the client into the depths, a levelling off, and an eventual return to the surface; this movement follows the line of the letter 'U', and is sometimes known as, 'the horse-shoe process'.

All the above counselling processes are useless when dealing with a traumatised client; the latter is not seeking 'growth as a person' (Rogers), nor interested in working to a goal (Egan), nor willing to dive into 'depths' that would terrify them! A completely different approach is required.

2.1 Group dynamics

The approach that I use is based on principles taken from group dynamics, not counselling; it is based on the dynamics (forces at work) that appear in both a group discussion and a group's development over time. My reason for moving in this direction is as follows.

At the heart of the matter in either group discussion or group development is *the power struggle* that takes place between opposites in conflict. It is this primitive struggle for power that blocks progress at meetings, and that leads groups to split into two or more factions. And since every traumatised person feels helpless, it follows that they too will home in on power or control like a bear seeking honey – especially when they come to you for counselling. In short, *counselling the abused is mostly a matter of working on the power struggle between you and the client*. And that is the concern of those involved with Group Dynamics.

By a power struggle I mean that, when the client presents him/herself as the little lamb which has been badly shocked, you have to keep in mind the large wild animal that is invariably behind them, ready to pounce. Behind every helpless person is a mountain of power; the quote, *"The tyranny of the minority is greater than the tyranny of the majority"* refers to the baby in the family; an infant is the most *helpless* member of the family, yet has the *power* to keep everyone awake all night long with its crying! The weaker the person, the greater the tyranny. And behind every terrified adult is a raging and unforgiving traumatised child struggling to get out and 'to get its own back' (which is why they make films like *'The Incredible Hulk'* or *'King Kong'*, a raging creature that goes on the rampage, yet can be soothed by a young woman).

This may explain why you as counsellor need to adjust your sights when dealing with a traumatised person. Instead of your usual professional focus on feelings, values, goals and actions, you now have to focus on the five senses, the instincts and, especially, on **danger**. Traumatised people are dangerous. What makes them so is their *terror*; their bodies are so full of trauma-induced chemicals that they no longer feel a simple emotion like *fear*; the latter is the feeling that alerts a person to the presence of danger in the environment. Without fear, they are blind to danger. Of course, they are forever *looking* for danger but simply can't see it when it comes. That's why they need a 'guide-dog' (or insurance agent) like you to be their eyes as they try to navigate their way through life. That's why you as their counsellor spend most of your time *looking for danger*, both to yourself and to the client; if you like, your theme song becomes, *"Every move you make, every step you take, I'll be watching you!"* This is not to say that you have to become paranoid. It only means that clients in their blindness are liable to 'get you' whether you're paranoid or not!

Speaking of danger, keep a look out for addiction. Once addiction in any form is 'put on the table' at a meeting of client and counsellor, it is a fairly safe bet that the issue for discussion will be trauma. This is also true in the case of a client who was not obviously traumatised, but who came from a family where one was an addict. What the client won't know – and what you need to know – is that he or she (the client) is probably now addicted to helping people! In short, if you live or work with either an addict or traumatised person, you become one. Both trauma and addiction are contagious dis-eases.

In other words, working with the traumatised is a 'high risk business'. If so, then the best way to work is to think of yourself and the other as forming a (business) **group**, albeit a small one, for a *meeting*, rather than thinking in terms of a one-to-one *relationship* between two individuals. Abused clients have already had their fill of so-called 'relationships' in the past, but don't feel particularly threatened by meetings.

2.2 Process in therapy

In the light of the above, it follows that any process you use when working with a traumatised client will be similar to that used in N. Ireland to reach a political agreement. Call it a 'peace process' if you like. Ultimately it will have to be about the power struggle. But first, it will have to be impersonal and business-like. In other words, a series of preliminary steps will have to be taken to prepare the 'climate' for a working environment. Secondly, the power struggle will have to be resolved through compromise and, finally, a series of steps will have to be arranged to ensure that any settlement can be maintained in the future. A general description of such steps can be found in any text on group dynamics.

The agenda

Crucial in this peace process is the working out of an agenda. Agree with your client in advance that the agenda should include:

- Their trauma story
- Their life story
- A written report at some stage on the traumatic event
- A study of traumatic symptoms
- Discussion about the effects of such symptoms on current life events
- Learning how to deal with such symptoms
- Ending the course of therapy.

Naturally, you don't put this in writing for the client to see; it would only scare them. Rather, you casually let them know what you are thinking, while encouraging them to go slowly with each point, and that it will all become clearer as both of you gradually move forward. Tell them that, if they feel up-tight about it all, so do you, but that you are prepared to go ahead with it – if they agree to 'give it a go'

Preliminaries

If both parties agree in general to an agenda, then begin

with the usual preliminaries about times for meeting, confidentiality etc. However, and especially in the case of those traumatised by sexual abuse, indicate that one of the conditions under which you work is that *you never make physical contact with a client* (I had a client who, on hearing this, ran out of the room! I waited for 15 minutes and she eventually returned. Later she explained that she thought my reason for making the statement was that I viewed her as an untouchable leper!) It can also be useful to mention contacts outside of the formal sessions; to that end, say, *"Please call me if it is an emergency. And please don't call me if it is not."* Then, if they phone you later, ask, *"Is this an emergency?"* and if it is not, say, *"Can you hold this till our next meeting?"*

All this may seem cold and formal, but remember that you are dealing with a very anxious person, and that the setting of boundaries lowers anxiety. The client may not like you for doing so (like the lady referred to above), but will feel safer in knowing precisely where you and they stand.

The Power Struggle

Once the preliminaries are over, both parties quickly move into the 'power struggle'. It begins once the client tells either their trauma story or life story. Of these, the former introduces the topic, and the latter reveals *patterns of abuse* in other areas of life. The life story is mostly an account of a life of abuse; it rarely makes mention of the many people who did not abuse the speaker. It is, however, useful to the client who can control the counselling situation by speaking on a topic in which they are the expert - abuse. To this extent, it is a power play by the client who, in presenting themselves as continually abused, implies that you, the counsellor, are but another potential abuser! It is also useful to you in that it frequently reveals the real and *original* traumatic event; the latter is 'just one of those things that happened on the day' to the client, but is most significant to you (clients may have had more than one trauma in the past but can have little memory of them; it is the original trauma that is significant, since all subsequent traumas are usually its consequences. In any case, *the earlier in life the trauma, the more severe the symptoms in later life*).

At this point, clients may want to 'go into' the trauma in more detail, and counsellors may have to 'pull back on the reins'. Your job as counsellor, of course, is to keep looking for *danger* since your client has a 'blind-spot' in this area.

Intervention

Part of the on-going power struggle requires that you make an intervention at some stage (as also happens when dealing with addictions). My way of intervening to stop a client from continually 'going round in circles' when telling their life story is to say, *"What happened to you in the past is history, and you are in danger of going around it in circles. It might be better for you to focus on your body here in the present."* I then go on to say that if they really want to look at the traumatic event, perhaps they should write out a report on the incident *in **the impersonal style** of the fairytale*; the latter was a tale that helped children deal with their terrors.

Written Trauma Report

Here are some guide-lines on how to write a report on a traumatic event in this style:

1) Do not use first names (*people in fairytales were identified by their work, not their names e.g. The King, The Princess, The woodcutter's son etc; any name used was more of a title or description - Snow White, Cinderella - than a*

name).

Instead, refer to yourself as 'the young boy' or 'young girl'; in other words, don't use the pronouns 'I' or 'me'.

2) Put yourself at the end of each sentence, not at the beginning.

For example, write, *"Johnson, the teacher, abused the young boy"* and not, *"I was abused by my teacher, Jack Johnson"*; the former is written in the impersonal style, the latter in the personal.

3) Focus on and describe what the abuser did, not on what you experienced. *"Johnson told the child to..."* and not, *"I had to...."*

4) Only report on 'what happened on the day' of the past event, not on the later consequences.

5) Record your story in a logical sequence, starting on the morning of the day and proceeding smoothly till sunset (don't jump about from morning to afternoon and then back to morning again).

In summary, clients write out their stories as if they were police officers recording what a witness had just told them.

Because such impersonal reports will be quite brief (usually one or two pages), the client may bring them into the next session and ask you to read them. Don't! Tell the client that you would rather hear them talk about what they've written. Some may insist that you read their material. If so, ask them to leave the letter on the table, and tell them that you will look at it after they've gone. But don't touch it in their presence.

The reason for not handling their letter, nor reading it

in their presence – nor, for that matter, giving them a hug or handshake etc - is that your job is to model *impersonal* behaviour; you've got to practice what you've been preaching. Keep yourself *at a distance* from both them and their traumas, and don't become too intimate with either.

If they want to give you a kiss on the cheek before leaving, remind them of the conditions under which both of you work - *'No contact'!* Never take the initiative in contacting them.

Getting things in perspective

Not only must you be impersonal, but you may have to coach the client on how to *speak* impersonally as well. One simple method is to correct their tendency to use the childish terms *Mum and Dad* when referring to their parents. Such terms are commonly used by many adults in this country, but only reinforce the illusion that the speaker is a child – whether traumatised or otherwise. The proper way for adult children to address their parents is to call them, *"Mother and Father"*.

Another useful tip is to challenge their use of the childish term *need*; "I need to get back to work this afternoon", "I need to have a talk with my son" Encourage them to switch from the *need* of the insecure child to the *want* of the adult; "I want to get back to work this afternoon" etc.

The most significant person in the past to them was - and still is - the abuser. To help them gain a sense of proportion, point out that to be angry with an abuser is to be angry with an emotional cripple; the latter could be defined as, 'An insignificant man who, when he abuses children, becomes significant in their estimation'. If so, then the abused *have the power* to reduce the abuser's significance to them. *"Stop looking on him as an evil giant, and start seeing him for what he really was – a pathetic gnome!"* In short, *"Why waste your life forever focusing on something insignificant?"*

To learn that their abuser was actually 'small' will shock your client. As I said earlier, shock occurs - as in this situation - when two truths collide; on the one hand, the truth is that the client really did - and still does - see the abuser as a giant with power, on the other hand, he now sees for the first time that the abuser really was 'small-minded' in more ways than one. But how can something be both big and small at the same time?

Part of the process of healing traumas is for the client to acknowledge the second truth as an adult, and to let go of the first as being merely the impression of a child.

Imagination

In the final stages of counselling, you may have to use your *imagination* when working with clients. This is because their imaginations have been closed-down by trauma. As a result, they can't imagine the past being different from how they once saw it, nor can they imagine the future being any different. Indeed, they will not see it as even possible (which is why so many believe that they won't live very long). This means that they will be dependent on your imagination to visualise the future.

Your job as counsellor is, not to visualise it as *possible* (as you would with an ordinary client), but to picture it as *desirable*. And you do this by first uncovering what the client secretly longs for, and then by encouraging her to take small steps in that general direction. For example, if she had always longed to be an artist some day, encourage her to take an art class as a preparation for later painting; don't assume that she will figure this out for herself. What is important is, not that she reaches the possible, but that she takes small steps towards the desirable. It is the *success in movement* that is significant. And, naturally, you praise and congratulate her for each small step taken – as you once did when your own children began to walk for the first time.

3. Conclusion

As a general rule, counsellors should refer the traumatised to others for obvious reasons. The problem, of course, is often, *"But where are those others?"* The simple truth is that there's a severe shortage of trauma counsellors. If so, experienced counsellors may have no alternative other than to deal with such clients themselves.

To that end, I have spelt out in this chapter several points worth remembering; if you want to move into trauma work, you will require at least some familiarity with the medical effects of trauma, with how people run a group meeting, and with how they develop as a group.

It is also worth remembering that trauma is primarily an *anxiety* state – even if the traumatised only speak about feeling depressed! And anxiety is a natural consequence of finding yourself helpless in a situation; for all practical purposes, anxiety and helplessness are interchangeable terms.

In turn, to be helpless means that you are in a situation where there's nothing much you can do about it – just like a child when faced with an adult abuser. And, later in life when that child grows up and runs into another situation where she feels helpless once more, all the memories from the past will flood back and *increase* her feeling of anxiety. This can even happen in the counselling room, especially when the counsellor tries to 'help' the client. For that is what the abuser once told the child – that he was only trying to help her, and that what he was doing was 'for her own good'! So, whatever you do, *don't try to help an abused client.* Rather, ask her to help you! As long as she is helping you, she will be fine; she will only go into depression at weekends, holiday times and when she comes to retirement; in short, when she is neither working nor helping you and others.

Instead of seeing yourself as a 'helper', view yourself as a board member going to a *meeting* and having to deal with a somewhat juvenile board member who is suffering from jet-lag after flying half way around the world. He will be edgy, easily irritated, unable to concentrate too long on heavy material, half in the room and half somewhere else on the other side of the universe, and liable to throw his brief-case at you if he gets too annoyed! Be professional. Be patient with him. And when you've done that, be even more patient. As the psychiatrist Judith Lewis Herman put it: think of a marathon rather than a sprint. Or think of a meeting that will go on and on for weeks, months and even years. (If you can't afford the time, then don't start working with the traumatised!) Time may destroy innocence, but it can also heal.

However, keep in mind that what the client needs and what you supply are two different things. They need to work on their symptoms through exercise or movement of some sort – and not just of the tongue! What you supply as counsellor is only part of what they need. The other part (dance, massage, karate, hard exercise, diet control etc) is supplied by others. But you certainly are in a position to encourage them to move in the right direction.

Also, given that trauma is a contagious dis-ease, it is even more necessary for you to make use of a supervisor; you will need someone else to keep an eye on whether you are becoming *addicted* to helping the abused or not. In this matter, it is extremely important that you do not trust your own judgement!

And, finally, don't worry if others make use of Cognitive Behavioural Therapy that can speed matters up considerably; you haven't been trained in this, so don't try to compete as a counsellor. Take your time, be soothing for a long time with the client, then become more impersonal as the months and even years pass by. In other words, you can empathise with the abused client *as long as they are not talking about their traumas* as such (e.g. when telling their life story), but once they begin to focus on evil things, then immediately adopt a more impersonal stance. This will not only facilitate the client, but will eventually make it easier for them to leave the meeting when ready to do so. As one traumatised woman in the States said, after lecturing on her abuse at 500 conferences, *"I stopped because I got bored!"* Nobody's traumatic story of child sex abuse is fascinating forever.

6. THE COMMUNICATION PROBLEM

Introduction

To paraphrase a quote from the writings of St. Thomas Aquinas, *"Fear brings us to counselling more than hope."* In other words, we hope for good things but fear evil things. Fear regards the aspect of difficulty more than hope does. *"And it is in matters of difficulty, especially when we distrust ourselves, that we take counsel."* I use this quote to illustrate what I've said earlier in this book, namely, that counselling, one of the 'modern' talking therapies, has been around for as long as humanity itself. In short and from a historical perspective, counselling was the art of exercising prudence when making a wise decision.

In some ways, it was unfortunate that Carl Rogers made use of the term *counselling* to describe the form of helping that he and his students had researched in a university setting; in their work, they had identified those characteristics of a helper that clients had found beneficial. While a valuable contribution, the discovery had the unfortunate consequence of drawing attention away from *prudence* and *wisdom,* and placing it entirely on *personal characteristics*; the latter, if you think about it, are no more than a means to an end. But, for Rogers (as for farmers), the means and the end were almost interchangeable terms;

'growth as a person' *was* the goal in counselling, and the personal characteristics of the counsellor represented the environmental 'climate' that made such growth possible; growth only occurs when the climate is suitable. If so, perhaps it would have been better had Rogers used the title *Growth therapy* when referring to his form of helping, rather than *Counselling.*

It was equally unfortunate that modern society accepted, for the most part, Rogers' understanding of counselling - for the simple reason that nobody could come up with a better description of what characterised a good helper.

It was even more unfortunate that society - especially that of socialist Europe – was unable or unwilling to accept the concept of the counsellor as a person *'employed by the system but not accountable to the system'* as originally envisaged in the States; such a concept was anathema to Europeans whose Constitutions created a bias towards *the group*, and who tended to concentrate more on the conservation of the group after two World Wars, than on the development of the person.

Indeed, they even viewed conservation itself in terms of protection, not enhancement; for example, conservationists might have desired to *enhance* the countryside, but governments preferred to *protect* it (until pressurised by public opinion) even though both used the same term, *conservation.*

That being the case, it was hardly surprising if European States approached counselling from an equally defensive position; they felt the need, not just to fit counsellors into the system for the protection of the group, but to introduce Codes of Ethics into the counselling profession for the protection of the individual. Protecting citizens from *internal* dangers (through policing) is nearly as big a business for Europeans as protecting citizens from *external* dangers (through soldiering) is for Americans.

This explains why the policy of the British government has been to focus on 'children in danger' and to leave 'children in need' to the voluntary sector; protection was what mattered, not enhancement. And social workers who dealt with children in danger were, in effect, their police force. It was not surprising, then, if social workers who became counsellors introduced their professionalism and protective Codes of Ethics into counselling. As a result, just as Rogers once diverted everyone's attention away from wisdom and directed it to personal characteristics, so Social Services have apparently and unintentionally diverted attention away from helping others and directed it towards the protection of individuals in a group; for Europeans with a policing mentality, what was important was the protection of the group, not the enhancement of the person. Call it 'the European way' if you like. (Social Services are beginning to speak about 'enhancement', but, as yet, seemingly only in association with its 'assessment' in cases involving child protection.)

I raise the above as a background to the question that confronts both counsellors and society when dealing with an abused individual: how do you communicate with someone who is an exiled immigrant (i.e. the traumatised) in their own country, who does not speak your language and who needs protection from you?

As worded, the question implies that there are two separate problems to be considered: the first lies in counselling, and the second lies in the social world.

I shall begin with the former.

1. The communication problem in counselling

In counselling, there is not only a process or movement over time, but also one taking place in each session. The latter refers to the *communication process* between two people, one in which each *informs* the other. This contrasts sharply with that of Rogers; for him, any communication process was no more than the outward expression of an inner kind of communication that tended to *form* both parties in a growth-full relationship. The difference between these opposing views of communication is that the former uses *logic* to inform, while the latter uses *myth* to form. And Carl Rogers was truly a great per-*form*-er when it came to counselling; like George Best, his skills were both mythical and legendary.

1.1 The mythical approach

At this point I need to divert a little to explain what I mean here by *myths*. The adult forms of fairytale, personal myths are the stories that you tell yourself and others to make sense of your history. They are a way of admitting that you are powerless to reconcile opposites, but still believe in the possibility of a solution. In other words, in such mythical stories it is more important to *believe* in a solution than to actually go out and find one. For example, everyone in Northern Ireland still believes in a solution after 30 odd years of trouble, but nobody seems to have found one after 30 odd years of searching. Still, if you have faith when you're powerless then at least you haven't lost hope!

Myth, be it social or personal, is different from history; the latter merely describes what happened in the past, but the former tells what *REALLY* happened in the past. History tries to focus on facts, and is open to the possibility that new facts might emerge that could change it. Myth, on the other hand, is always closed and absolute: *"It is so because I say that it is so!"*

Myths also differ from fairytales. The latter are used by society to convince children that the desirable is possible i.e. that they, too, can 'live happily ever-after' if they are as good as the characters in the tale. By contrast, myths are used by society to convince adults that the possible is believable i.e. that they, too, can 'live on after death' (as did Jack in the latest movie of *The Titanic*). In short, fairytales explain life to children, while myths explain death to adults (that's why all good myths – like that of *Romeo and Juliet*, or that of *The Titanic* – end with the death of the hero who tried to reconcile opposites). Accordingly, when I say that clients in counselling use myth, I mean that they, too, tell a story that involves two people in conflict (themselves and another), and that they still believe in a solution even though they've never found one as yet.

To get back to the point I was making earlier about Rogers, I should add that it is valid to use either logic or myth when communicating. For example, a scientist when addressing a convention, will speak in a logical manner to inform the audience of his findings, whereas popular tabloids tend to present myths to form their customers; the former is interested in 'the truth', the latter in creating a story that is more 'interesting' than true; truth is only important in so far as it adds to interest (to sell a product, you can't afford to either bore or scare people with truth!)

1.2 The logical approach

It was Gerard Egan with his business-like approach who used logic to restore *wisdom* to its rightful place in counselling. While acknowledging the need for 'mothering skills' as implied in Rogers' approach, Egan emphasised 'fathering skills' (concreteness, confrontation and immediacy) that are required to *move* the person towards helping themselves. And, whereas Rogers viewed *movement* as a purely inner and *organic* activity (as found in vegetables and, indeed, in babies), Egan saw it as a *developmental* activity (found, say, in older children and adolescents who often require a push from their father, encouraging them to separate from - and stop clinging to -

their mothers, while preparing them to leave home eventually).

Both forms of counselling are useful in different situations. The more damaged a client is, the more helpful is an approach that uses the *soothing* skills of Carl Rogers. The less damaged s/he is, the more useful the assertive (or *protective*) approach of Gerard Egan.

There is, however, a difficulty with both approaches when counsellors from either school of thought have to deal with a traumatised client, especially an adult who has been sexually abused as a child. This difficulty is a communication one.

As indicated above, the Egan approach works from the assumption that both parties in the counselling relationship are adults who can *communicate logically*. Furthermore, Egan was only interested in the client's story as a background to what was *really* important, namely, identifying the problem, converting it to a goal, and pursuing that goal to a satisfactory conclusion.

By contrast, Rogers believed that the counsellor should follow the client's story - and even 'go into it'- through empathy in order to see the world as the client sees it. The 'world', of course, *is the story itself.* And, like all stories, is mythical; it describes a conflict of opposites that created a crisis in the client's development at specific moments of time, the main ones being: birth, childhood, adolescence, love, work and death (all myths centre on these themes). In other words, Rogers and his clients *communicated through the adult language of myth*.

1.3 Fairytale

Counsellors trained in either of the above approaches are guaranteed to experience difficulty with untreated traumatised adult clients who do not communicate in either the language of logic or that of myth. Instead, they communicate in *the language of the fairytale*; not only do they *act* and *speak* like a much younger person, but also *think* in the same manner (which is why you can't use complicated words or adult terms when speaking with them about the human body). For example, traumatised people tend to view the police as 'pigs' in certain countries, and as 'wolves' in others. Clearly, the viewers are making use of the fairytale, *The three little pigs and the big, bad wolf,* not as an adult metaphor, but because they actually see the police in this childish way – due to trauma, of course!

Or take the case of a woman (sexually abused as a child) who shows her counsellor a hand-drawn sketch of a hideous alien and says, "That's me!" Then, in a later session, says, "My father always called me his 'little princess'". It takes a certain level of training for the counsellor to connect these separate incidents – and to realise that the fairytale is *Beauty and the Beast.* In other words, if counsellors have no idea that the traumatised *think* like children, they will only be horrified by the initial sketch, and charmed by the later analogy; they will not make the connection. As a result, there will be 'a failure to communicate'.

The truth is that the traumatised revert to fairytales, not just because their adult myths about life have been wrecked by trauma but, primarily, because their bodies are flooded with extra chemicals that leave them reacting not unlike alcoholics; the more alcohol in the system, the younger they seem to become; indeed, at the end of day, they can end up crawling home while needing their diapers changed! In a similar manner, the more severe the trauma, the younger the person appears to become. As one 50 year-old survivor of former child abuse said to me, *"People don't know that I'm seven years old".*

1.4 Counselling through fairytale

Once you grasp that you as counsellor are dealing with a child – no matter what age they actually are as adults – you will then understand why it is so easy to work with the abused; as a parent, you have had lots of experience in raising children. You will know exactly why the traumatised act so 'weirdly', why they have difficulty concentrating, why they are so impulsive, why their moods swing so dramatically, why they are more interested in castles, gardens and 'messing about', than in coming home on time, why their expectations fluctuate so much, and why they are so terrified of responsibility. You will also know why your tone of voice has to be soft and soothing so as not to aggravate their nervous system, and why you as counsellor (mother) have to remain inwardly still when surrounded by their fury and terror.

You will not be surprised then if, in the counselling situation, an apparently adult woman will suddenly speak as a Princess (*"Why am I so different from other people?"*) and, a few minutes later, may suddenly turn into a Witch (*"How dare you think like that!"*) They are clearly 'acting-out' some inner fairytale. Other samples are: *"I don't want people to see me"* or, *"I wish I was invisible!"* (the Cheshire Cat in *Alice in Wonderland*), or, *"I'm afraid to move in case I go to pieces"* (Humpty Dumpty), or, *"I'm always in a hurry but end up in a hole!"* (The White Rabbit). The list is endless.

Logical adults, of course, will view the above as no more than the ordinary adult's use of childish metaphor or analogy. If anything, they will say that such abused people are adults playing the part of a child. The truth, however, is the very opposite. Those who were abused as children remain children – like Peter Pan – but grow up *pretending to be adults*; they function on the outside like every other adult but, inside, continue to be a terrified child in hiding.

Or, to use the language of the theatre, their mask may be that of the adult, but the hidden actor is still a child.

1.5 The moral language of the fairytale

To a large extent, putting things in perspective means keeping an eye on the client's use of terms that refer to space. For example, when arrested or accused, most adult abusers respond, *"What's the big deal? We were only having a little fun!"* Notice their use of the spatial terms, *big and little,* to describe respectively the deal and the fun. The same spatial terms will be used by a traumatised client for the simple reason that they refer to morality as children see it.

Adults view morality in terms of *good and bad* or even *wise and foolish* as we shall see later. Children, however, have a different sense of morality, one that is viewed in terms of *size.* That's because children occupy a very small space in the grand scheme of things; their bodies are small by comparison to those of adults. It is this sense of being small that leaves them feeling vulnerable in a world of 'giants'. In short, for the very young, big is bad (since big people can punish) and small, being the opposite, is good.

This explains why in fairytales, the immoral are big (the Big Bad Wolf) and the moral are small (Three Little Pigs). For the same reason giants are bad, and Curly Wee is good. And since traumatised people think like children, it should be no surprise if they too use spatial terms to describe morality and experiences: *"I live in a little house"*, *"I just love to bits my wee son!"* *"My biggest fear is becoming pregnant!"* *"This has all been a big change for me".* It makes sense, then, for the trauma counsellor to assume that the child abuser was - and still is - a 'big' person in the client's thinking, and that the latter sees himself or herself as 'small' when talking with you.

It is of further interest to note that *big* can be subdivided into *great and large*. Both terms appear to have originally been used to describe trees; a great tree was a tall one, while a large tree was a wide one. Clearly, greatness was associated with masculine height, whereas largeness was associated with feminine width. Take, for example, *"He's a great wee man"* and, *"She's a large wee woman"*. While the 'wee' in both instances refer to the person's goodness (just as, "He's a *little* devil!" means he is good), the terms *great* and *large* clearly have a sexual connotation. Another example: a 'great heart' refers to masculine courage (even in women), while a 'large heart' refers to feminine caring (even in men). Because these terms are linked with sex, and because women cannot be seen to be inhumanly evil by a child, it is hardly surprising if the masculine *great* is used to describe evil, but never the feminine *large*. For example, *"She's a great liar!"* is socially acceptable, but not, *"She's a large liar!"* Nor should it be surprising to learn that a larger or wider view of things is to be encouraged as a way of coping with the greatness or evil of abuse at the hands of 'bigger' people.

In the light of the above, you as a trauma counsellor would be wise to encourage abused clients to take 'small' steps when moving towards a 'wider' vision of 'what happened' in the past. And as mentioned previously, your task is also to reduce the *size* of the abuser in the client's memory from giant to gnome. Naturally, if at any stage the client responds, *"That would be a big step for me"*, you will know what is meant – that the step is too frightening and dangerous. This becomes particularly true when it comes to 'letting go' of the past.

Given, then, that the language of the abused is couched in terms of childish imagery, and that their moral language is based on spatial concepts, it follows that whenever you *meet* with such a client, you may find yourself attending, not a board-meeting as such, but the Mad Hatter's Tea not a board-meeting as such, but the Mad Hatter's Tea Party – with you playing the part of Alice, while the client plays all the other roles! As already implied in this book, child sexual abuse is a social problem. As such, the difficulty it raises for the child concerns *social roles* that s/he is expected to play in life – if any. This means that the issue in therapy is not 'person' but 'roles' – hence the need for the impersonal, and the equal need to focus on *the social*, not the personal. Ultimately what abused people have to learn are social skills necessary for dealing with their enemy – society.

2. The communication problem in society

Post Traumatic Stress Disorder is a *medical* condition that has *psychological* side-affects; it primarily affects the *body*, and secondarily the *group* (a distinction previously referred to on p.25 of this book). If so, its treatment is primarily the responsibility of the medical profession, and only secondarily is it the work of psychologists and social workers. I think it important to state this since so much confusion seems to exist in the mind of the general public.

The difficulty for the medical profession is that research into the human brain and central nervous system (all of which are affected by trauma) is still at an early stage of development; you can't simply open up a living brain and experiment with it! As a consequence of this gap in medical knowledge, psychologists and their associated social workers have moved in, and have almost 'cornered the market', so to speak, in the treatment of psychological trauma; by way of analogy, the second team is now playing the game since the first team was delayed in coming. Having said that, it is important to add that the contribution of psychologists has been truly remarkable.

The problem, in turn, for psychologists and social workers is that their case-loads are ever increasing as the

Consequently, a situation of triage now exists, and to prevent matters from deteriorating further, society is now turning to counsellors (or 'the third team' as I call them) for that extra bit of help needed.

This may be necessary, but it is like opening Pandora's Box. As mentioned above, counselling throughout history dealt with wisdom, not trauma. Furthermore, it has tended in more recent times to become separate from wisdom – thanks to Rogers – and now includes a diverse spectrum of professions ranging from psychotherapists at one end, to advice-givers at the other.

And while some therapists at the upper-end of counselling (e.g. psychotherapists) may have knowledge about trauma, those with a Diploma in Counselling usually have little, while those with only a Certificate in Counselling - together with all advice-givers - have none. In short, the social world has a problem in trying to communicate with the adult victims of child sex abuse, be it from ignorance, lack of resources or incompetence.

3. Conclusion

One important lesson I have learned from trauma is that it is *contagious*. Not only does it affect those who suffered child sex abuse, but also everyone who cares about them; this is true from the top ranks of Church and State to the lower end of the social scale. All become traumatised (though in different degrees). This means that all will react *as untreated 'victims' react*; for example, they will find themselves unable to forget 'what happened', feel betrayed by a 'Judas' who was so evil, become depressed, worry about how other people see them, be tempted to adopt the code of the abusive family, *"Don't wash your dirty linen in public"*, have difficulty imagining how things might change, focus heavily on morality rather than on religion, focus on the future with increasing anxiety, and adopt, "Never again!" as their battle-cry etc. etc.

And just as untreated individuals become addicted to soothing activities such as smoking, eating, drinking, gambling etc, so too will society become addicted; it will become addicted to *helping the 'victims'*. An example of this addiction is where someone might say, "*We in the Church have so much to offer them* (the abused), *but they just won't listen to us!*" Such language is but a reflection of the arrogance of ignorance. It takes a lot of humility to face both those who suffered and the truth. It takes humility to admit that *those who have learned how to cope with their traumas have so much to offer a traumatised society.*

What the abused everywhere want is to receive a hearing in which they can carry out their God-given mission, namely, to testify *that they had witnessed, long ago, the abuse of an innocent person in the form of a child.* And it makes little difference if the abuser had been a man or a woman.

What they also need, in return, is lots of support from the social world. Unfortunately, as I said above, the social world was shocked by the news of abuse and, as a consequence of trauma, was rendered dumb, unable to hear the real truth, and unable to see anything other than 'compensation' (in all my many years of working with the adult survivors of child sex abuse, I have never met a single instance where an abused adult was *even thinking* about compensation; *nobody who thinks like a child is interested in compensation.* All they ever wanted was what terrified and damaged children seek throughout the world - to be heard and comforted by their mothers i.e. social support).

Of course, there is no doubt that the abused can be influenced by the media or by unethical therapists who are in a position to *plant* the notion of compensation in their minds - although it is more likely that most therapists will steer their clients towards seeking *justice*; in this case, compensation becomes more a consequence or result of litigation than an effect; the abused only want to be heard but may have to make-do with such compensation as the lesser of two evils.

In other words, we initially refer adults who had been formerly abused to therapists and counsellors for treatment. That treatment consists in helping them to deal with their 'deafness' (their inability to listen to those adults who remind them of their abuser), their 'dumbness' (their inability to speak about the unspeakable) and their 'blindness' (their inability to see or understand 'what happened' to them).

Having been treated, those same adults then return to a society that no longer wants to hear anything further about abuse (is deaf), no longer wants to talk about it (is dumb) and who can't see the point in anyone even raising the topic, and who view those who do as 'trouble-makers' (is blind). In short, they return to a traumatised society, but one that has no awareness of its own need for treatment! Clearly, there is going to be a serious 'failure to communicate'!

Ordinarily, most treated adults focus their attention on wider environmental problems; they appreciate that, just as their bodies as children had once been abused, so also the planet is being currently abused by rampant capitalism. This being the case, they soon become conservationists seeking to enhance the world, rather than policemen trying to protect it; for example, they want the rain forests to grow and develop, and not just stop more trees from being felled. They believe that a positive attitude is better for the earth in the long term, than a negative attitude in the short term. Likewise, when dealing with a traumatised society, they believe that a positive and helping attitude is better than a negative and defensive one.

It is understandable, then, if such treated adults feel somewhat aggrieved with some of their fellow sufferers who have opted instead for a *defensive and protective* litigation when dealing with a traumatised society. To seek impersonal justice is one thing. To go public through personal media appearances is an entirely different matter. One can only wonder how such a narrow and *personal* stance can be reconciled with the wider and *cosmic* vision of those who have been properly treated. How does litigation enhance the planet? Does it even enhance society? Does litigation lead to a better protection for children? Does it result in a social change of heart?

Let me give you an example of what a 'treated' person looks like. A middle aged and single lady, who had been raised in an Industrial School from the age of 3 to 16, came to me for counselling. While not sexually abused in the school, she had experienced physical and emotional abuse. As part of her work with me, she wrote out her life story by hand, then went to computer classes to learn how to type and to put her writing into print. In her finished manuscript, she recorded that one of her childhood dreams had been to become an authoress someday. I asked her would she mind if I showed her text to a publishing company. She gave me permission and I duly handed the work over to one such company. The response was positive; the publisher believed there was a ready market for such material. I passed the information to the lady - who, by then, had long since completed therapy with me - and asked her if she wanted to go ahead with the publication. She thought for a moment, then said, *"No! If what happened in the past shocked me, it will shock everyone who reads about it, and I don't want anyone to go through what I had to go through. I'd prefer if my book went to some place where researchers could use it in the future"*. To me, that kind of social consciousness and capacity for mercy is what I associate with a 'properly treated' survivor of abuse.

It is only through a better understanding of our communication problems that we – both survivors and society – will find a solution to shared problems.

7. THE INCREDIBLE JOURNEY

In the previous chapter, I indicated that without some understanding of how a child's mind works, it becomes impossible to really follow those who have been traumatised and who now think as a child. In this chapter, I want to examine some of the themes that are relevant when counselling the sexually abused, themes that do not usually appear in regular counsellor training. I also want to consider the attitude that a trauma counsellor must adopt when dealing with such clients.

I will present the above in three steps that correspond to the stages of development of a person, namely, from childhood through adolescence to adulthood. I like to think of it as the incredible journey from hope through confidence to love.

1. Hope and desire

From a psychological perspective, hope is the first thing an infant learns from being breast-fed. The words used to describe what a child feels before he is fed - *hunger, desire, craving, and longing* - and after he is fed - *fulfilled* (being filled full) and *successful* (filling an empty space as in 'succeeding someone in office') - are precisely the same words used to describe *hope*; the latter is the hunger or desire to be fulfilled and successful in life.

As a consequence, it is true to say that hope is *the foundation* upon which later psychological structures are built; *faith (confidence)* is the first floor of the building, and *love (choosing or making a decision)* becomes the second floor. In other words, you can have hope (the foundation) without faith and love (the building), but you can't have faith and love without hope; once the latter is destroyed, everything else collapses. It is important for you to grasp this should you choose to work with a traumatised client. The latter will usually describe what happened to them as 'incredible'; "*I can't **believe** that anyone would do such a thing!*" If so, you are in danger of taking from this that the core issue is faith or confidence, rather than hope. To do so is to miss the point.

Ordinarily, and in the 'maintenance' world of helping, counsellors are those who assist clients to repair the first and second storeys of their house after they've lost *confidence* in themselves. Confidence is based on knowledge in that the more you know, the more confident you feel. But when you don't know what you need to know in order to make a decision, you lose confidence – and can't make a decision! All this is but part of the normal process of living.

Traumatised people, by contrast, are children for all practical purposes, a point that should be clear from the previous chapter. The major issue for them - as for all young children - is **HOPE**. For this reason, psychiatrists view the *disordering of hope* as the greatest damage arising from the trauma of abuse; damage to the foundation is greater than damage to the entire psychological super-structure above it. When hope is damaged, *the house built upon it cannot be repaired*; it can only be rebuilt. This explains why 'repair' people such as counsellors are of little use to someone whose entire world has collapsed and who describes the experience as incredible.

This also explains why you as trauma counsellor put your focus largely on **hope**. And to do that you look at how growing children develop it – through the fantasy of fairytales; *fantasy creates hope*. Adults may get confidence from *myths* (using Carl Rogers' approach), and may gain the ability to make decisions by the use of *logic* (using Gerard Egan's approach), but young children take hope from their memory of recent success and from using their *imagination*.

1.1 Imagination

The problem for the traumatised, however, is that the images in their memories are horrific and their imagination has been shut down by trauma as we saw in chapter 5 when considering the ideas of van der Kolk. It is this combination of too many bad memories and not enough imagination that leaves the traumatised adult feeling so hopeless.

But trauma also shuts down that part of the brain that deals with planning and rationalising. To counter this, Cognitive Behavioural Therapy was designed to promote rational thinking. If so, why not use 'Imagination Therapy' to kick-start the client's back into life? I mean, when a baby cries, mothers know how to *soothe* them. Equally, they know how to *distract* them with rattles etc. Either method works. If so, then use *your* imagination to distract child-like clients from horrible memories. After all, children are moved by *images*, not ideas.

In the light of the above, you might be wise to focus, less on talking about ideas (which research has shown to have limited affect on the traumatised in any case), and more on encouraging the client to **MOVE** into creating images, paintings, collages or photographs *that symbolise order;* such images, being positive, are very useful in distracting clients from the horrible images in their memory. When working with traumatised clients, *talk to their eyes*, not to their ears.

1.2 Eyes

As indicated earlier, you work primarily with the client's five senses. Of these, the eyes are probably the most important. This is particularly true when trying to put distance between themselves and their nightmares. As merchants discovered long ago, communicating with customers close-by required the use of two organs – *mouth and ears* – for speech purposes, but when communicating long distance, two other organs were required - *hand and eye* – for writing purposes. In time, this association of 'distance' with 'writing' explains why you say to clients, "*If you want to put distance between yourself and your memories, put them in writing!*" If they want to take control, tell them to use their eyes and hands (this also explains why, in business companies, managers are forever issuing vision statements in order to handle their business), rather than their tongue and ears. It also explains what I said above, '*talk to their eyes, not to their ears*'.

1.3 Images

'Talking to another's eyes' means speaking about images, not ideas. It means visualising in language the images in your head so that the client can *see* them. But the key image to portray when speaking about order is that of *beauty*; after all, as we know, beauty soothes. So, ensure that the images you communicate to your client are of beauty, and not horror. As I said earlier, trauma work consists in *taming* the wild animal within, and a beautiful girl certainly tamed King Kong – as surely as did Beauty tame the Beast in the original fairytale. Accordingly, you ensure that your counselling room is full of beauty. You surround yourself with beauty and, by so doing, model what the client has to do.

None of this should be difficult for you since you've been trained to empathise as a counsellor. Images move people. And talking in an imaginative way is precisely what we mean by being empathic; a statement is only empathic if it moves the listener, and not just informs them. This is why you try to see *images* of real life rather than form abstract ideas about it. To that end, you pick up the client's *similes, analogies and metaphors* ("I felt like a volcano of anger"), and then use these to make a mental *picture* of what you've heard. Such pictures, in turn, will *move* you; they will create in you the desire to reach out and 'touch' the client by your response, *"You felt as though you were about to erupt and show the world what he did to you?"* It is not the *truth* in such a comment that moves the client; it is the **desire** *that she senses in you* that touches her.

In other words, trauma work involves a lot of acting as in a theatre; such a performance assists the abused to work out what *role* they should adopt when dealing with others. It is the *desire of a mother* that instils desire in her child, and that plays such a powerful influence on the latter when deciding what social role to play in later life. And it is your purpose as a trauma counsellor to make the other realize what you are saying by *desiring* to instil in her what you see in yourself. In short, desire breeds action.

2. The Wise One

It may be noticed in this book that I have used two paradigms - that of Priest and that of Wise One - and that neither is particularly female. I have also indicated that the Priest is a masculine figure since he symbolises the impersonal Deity who *protects* (whereas the feminine symbolises that which is *good* – the family and social world). From a child's perspective, only a father deity can protect from an equally masculine evil (or Satan); as I said, for a child to think of his mother as either evil or capable of changing into some form of monstrous beast is simply too frightening to be considered; mother must always be close, intimate and completely human in form.

However, it becomes an entirely different matter when we examine the paradigm of Wise One. Given that 'things' referred to the public world, while 'person' referred to the private one, it follows that two different standards of *behaviour* were required for groups and for individuals. The Code for a group became known as a Code of Ethics, whereas that for a person became known as a Code of Morality. This means that a Company can be accused of acting in an unethical manner, but only an individual can be accused of acting immorally.

The main point to notice in all this is that both terms, *ethics* and *morality*, referred to human activity, not to religion as such - although it seems true to say that most people link moral codes with religion to such an extent that they equate one with the other. Furthermore, human activity becomes complicated by the fact that it involves two sexes. And while the paradigm of Wise One was associated with general human *behaviour*, it was felt that distinctions were required to accommodate sexual roles. This led to the splitting of the original paradigm into two parts that seem to reflect the preference of parents in a family; most enjoy seeing their sons as heroic, but would prefer if their daughters were wise!

2.1 The Hero

In his book, *The Cry for Myth*, Rollo May argues that the hero represents the soul of the community in that his task is to uphold its moral and ethical values. A hero is not necessarily someone who does extraordinary deeds; rather he carries out his ordinary activities in what might be called extraordinary circumstances. By so doing, he remains faithful to the values of the community. In short, he is a myth in action.

From this it follows that, where there are no more heroes, there is no community. For that reason Rollo May regrets the current dearth of heroes, and their replacement by 'celebrities', people who represent no known values or standards of action, but who excel at 'strutting their stuff'; they replace ethics with style. To be cynical about heroes in this manner is to be cynical about ethics.

What is interesting in the above is the reference to the hero as representing the 'soul' of the community. If so, where there are no more heroes, the 'soul' of the community is gone in the sense that there is no longer any sense of ethics or morality in that community, and that, as a result, there is no more community.

Possibly for a similar reason, some experts refer to child sex abuse as, *"The murder of the soul"*. While damaging the hopes of a child, it equally affects the beliefs and love of every adult close to that child. This means that the 'sense of ethics and morality' is replaced by a violent and obsessive *addiction* to ethics and morality. As I said earlier, *"Evil attaches"* and the evil of child sexual abuse certainly locks all concerned into an addictive attachment to *behaviour* and morality – not to religion as such. If anything, the addiction to morality is a complete distraction from religion. Instead of focusing on God and Saints, the abused community is in danger of switching its focus to avenging *heroes*, the symbols of the community's ethical and moral standards - as can be seen on the gable walls of working class areas throughout the North of Ireland.

2.2 Wise Woman

In most societies, according to Rollo May, *women symbolise community*. It is women who oppose death by focusing on life. And while warrior-heroes might die gloriously in defence of ethics and morality, women know it is wiser *to live* an ethical and moral life.

Wisdom, however, consists in more than recognising that war precedes peace. It involves the creation of a home, a community and a world in which everyone can be heard – thereby uprooting the need to make war in the first place. It consists in maintaining that world through the acceptance and practice of communal values. Where wisdom is missing, the community too often can view values as imposed from without or from the past, rather than reflecting what really matters in life. And without wisdom, there is no guarantee that the hero is anything other than a fool.

What I'm saying, in other words, is not that men are heroic and women wise, but that both sexes symbolise different aspects of the paradigm of Wise One - heroism and wisdom - when dealing with human behaviour. If men ran the world, then everyone's focus would be on the hero's battle with the cowardly villain. Equally, if women ran the world, the focus would be on the wise woman's struggle with the foolish virgin. In other words, the opposite of the hero is, not the wise woman, but the coward, and the opposite of the wise woman is, not the hero, but the fool. Again, in saying this I am not implying that men are cowardly or women foolish! Rather I'm saying that heroism without wisdom is foolishness, and wisdom without heroism is cowardice. In short, the paradigm of Wise One for *both* sexes requires a balance between heroism and wisdom so as to avoid accusations of being either a coward or fool.

Those two terms, *coward* and *fool*, will appear in most counselling sessions with an abused client: "*I didn't have the courage to say anything at the time*", "*I felt so ashamed about what happened*" "*I was too scared to do anything*", "*I hadn't the nerve to tell my parents"* and again, *"He fooled me into thinking he was my friend"*, *"Looking back on it, I must have been an idiot!"* *"People think I was stupid to let it happen"*, *"I feel like a complete fool talking about it"* *"He made a jackass out of me!"*

2.3 Implications for counsellors

I have written the above for you should you be faced with clients who have been exposed to the reality of evil. Few clients will admit this. That's why they are happy to talk about themselves in the moral terms of *coward* and *fool* rather than in the more religious term of *evil*. Like children, they believe that they *caused* another person to act in an evil manner. And it is this childish tendency to *personalise causality* that is behind their use of the terms *coward* and *fool*; the latter are but one step away from *evil*. So, if they use such terms in your presence, make no mistake about what they are saying, namely, that they see themselves as 'evil' in their person. They most certainly are not talking about their level of social courage or that of their personal I.Q!

I have also written the above for you when dealing with ordinary (not traumatised) clients. You have been trained to adopt a non-judgemental (amoral) approach and it is the latter that I think needs to be considered in the light of the above.

In the film, *Enemy of the State*, Gene Hackman (as former CIA agent) whispered to Will Smith (as lawyer) about to enter a mafia restaurant, *"Either you are incredibly smart or incredibly stupid!"* which, if you think about it, meant that the lawyer was either a clever hero or a fool. Equally, it could have meant that Hackman was either cowardly or wise! The point being that both characters in the movie were faced with a situation that called for the taking of *a risk*.

That, of course, is the situation with which you have to deal when working with ordinary clients. Most counsellors in such circumstances adopt the non-judgemental stance of Carl Rogers and Gerard Egan, meaning that they refrain from passing judgment on the *goodness or badness* of the client's actions. However, 'good and bad' are moral terms associated with the hero. They are not terms associated with the wise woman; in the latter case, the appropriate terms are *wise and foolish*. Accordingly, when rejecting the moral judgement of someone's behaviour in terms of the hero, does this mean that a moral judgement worded in terms of the wise woman must also be rejected? If you follow the principles of Carl Rogers, the answer to that question would clearly be, "Yes!" That's because Rogers was interested in growth rather than wisdom. And there is little doubt that many in the States go to therapy for 'growth' in the form of personal development.

However, here in Europe most people go to counselling in search of a wisdom that might be useful when dealing with others; the emphasis is on social - and not just personal - development. I, for one, never speak to clients in terms of 'good and bad' or 'right and wrong', but have no hesitation in using the terms 'wise and foolish' when talking with them about their behaviour. It is not that I judge them with a statement. Rather, I word it as a question, *"Were you wise in doing that?"* And instead of calling them a fool, I ask, *"Were you wise in the head when doing that?"* I mean, if you ask a question, who can accuse you of making a judgement?

"Aha!" will reply my critics, *"But in your heart you were judging them!"* To all such legal-minded people, I can only respond that no client has ever accused me of being judgemental when asked about their level of wisdom. If so, then to those counsellors who refrain from every known form of judgement I can only say, *"Either you are incredibly*

wise, or incredibly cowardly!" The point being that, either way, your credibility is open to question.

Which brings me to my final section in this chapter on the incredible.

3. Love and Truth

In previous chapters I referred to two of Rogers' characteristics of a helper – *congruence* (genuineness) and *empathy*. His third was *love*. This meant that he and his students had shown how the level of help received by a client depended on the level of loving care shown by the helper.

However, in the States at the time, 'love' had many meanings – mostly associated with sex. Accordingly, Rogers and his team of researchers sought an alternative term, and finally adopted the awkward sounding, *'unconditional positive regard'*. Clearly the 'positive regard' referred to the love of a mother for an infant. I say this since 'regard' implies that you are looking at someone *below* you on the social scale ('respect' implies looking at an equal, and 'esteem' implies looking at someone above you in society). If so, then 'positive regard' describes the loving way a mother might look at her child.

3.1 Unconditional problems

Rogers understood unconditional positive regard to mean 'acceptance' of the client. But then he had previously described genuineness or congruence in a similar way; to be genuine, the client had to *accept* themselves and not be a phoney playing a role. Now, the counsellor had to be equally accepting of the client, that is to say, without any conditions of worth. In the latter situation, this meant that the counsellor had to go along with the *feelings* of the client without conditions; 'bad' feelings were now as acceptable as 'good' feelings.

Unfortunately, the term 'acceptance' also carries connotations of giving consent, or of going along with the *desires* of another. And once again Rogers' blindness to the existence of evil apparently prevented him from seeing how his version of 'acceptance' could be so easily misinterpreted and misused by others – as mentioned in chapter 3 when speaking about sexual activity by therapists in California.

Unconditional acceptance only exacerbated the problem. A condition assumes a duality, namely, that an antecedent precedes a consequent; something must first happen before something else takes place. By way of illustration, a student must first pass his exams before entry into college; the passing of an exam is the condition, and the entry into college the consequence. If so, then 'unconditional' in this instance means that no exam is required for college entry; it means there is no antecedent.

Without any antecedent, *unconditional* human love amounts to unlimited acceptance of another which, while ideal, is unreal for most mortals. While clearly intended by Rogers to mean 'unbounded' as in a mother's love for her child, it can also mean 'infinite' as in God's love for His creation; for example, *unbounded* means leaving the boundary or limits of the earth at the start of a space journey, whereas *infinite* suggests there is no limit to space - and no end to the trip! By removing the conditions from 'positive regard', Rogers effectively triggered in the client the desire for God's love, but eliminated the possibility of success in ever finding it in the counsellor!

Possibly for this reason, Carkhuff, Egan and others began to modify the terminology used by Rogers. The 'regard' that the latter had associated with love and care was replaced by a 'respect' associated more with trust and confidence. And secondly, this respect tended to be fairly conditional: "*I will respect you to the extent that you respect yourself!*"

All of which leads to the question: how do you look at the adult client who has been sexually abused as a child? With regard? With respect? Or with esteem? The simple answer is – *with humility*!

3.2 Humility

To understand the latter, it is necessary to go back to the five senses of the body previously considered. This time, our focus will be on the ear. The function of the ear is to hear and, in the case of a child, to hear what adults say about danger and safety. This need for hearing led to the coining of the term 'obedience' (a combination of the Latin, *ob* and *audire*: 'on account of hearing'). Originally it meant that both parents and children had to listen to each other. Unfortunately with the passing of time, two things happened. First, the military model of obedience became predominant when dealing with children and, secondly, the psychological model of obedience became dominant when it came to adults.

The military model demanded that those in the lower ranks must listen to their officers, but that those in charge could only listen to those above them in the social scale. When this model was applied to the family, it meant that children had to listen to their parents, but that the latter had no obligation to listen to them.

The psychological model added to the above by demanding that adults must listen to their 'superior' conscience - their 'true inner self' - when dealing with children. The understanding was that the 'true inner self' was to be formed, in turn, by society, be it Church or State. The end result was that children were 'to be seen but not heard' in Western Civilization, and that the obedience expected of them was no more than a caricature of what had been originally intended. It also meant that children who grew up in homes where nobody listened to them, began to dissociate. On the one hand, they learned how to conform with the instructions of adults and, on the other hand, how to turn inwards to a fairytale world of imagination in which to feel at home. It was hardly surprising that many as adults came later for counselling; even the therapist, Rollo May, was struck by the fact that so many of his clients described themselves as having come from a home where nobody listened to them!

Both the longing to be heard and the tendency to conform left such children vulnerable to any adult predator out hunting children for sexual or power purposes; if he could not get their cooperation *by listening* to them, he could always get them to conform *by ordering* them. It really was that simple. The 'art' of the successful paedophile lay in identifying, not the most attractive children, but those who came from families where the parents were strict disciplinarians - that is to say, 'teachers' and 'preachers' who never had time to listen to their children - or from families where the parents were either physically or emotionally absent.

Is it not strange that what successful paedophiles have always known remains unknown to the rest of society? Or could it be that society prefers to hold on to its caricature of obedience at any cost? Most certainly every child who was abused knows that, for him or her, the issue when meeting an adult predator was *obedience*, not chastity. After all, it had been drilled into the child that 'adults know best', so 'do what you're told'. Accordingly, when the wolf dressed as a sheep said, *"This is for your own good"*, the child knew exactly how to react: *"Do what you're told!"* In short, the child practiced obedience in the distorted manner in which he or she had been trained.

3.3 The Child as Hero
The child also practiced that obedience in an

extraordinary situation. By so doing, s/he followed the moral standards of the family and society. But the upholding of these in circumstances of extreme difficulty is the very definition of a 'hero' as already noted. If so, then why is it that no reference is ever made in this country to the heroism of such children? Is it that society is more interested in religion than morality, that saints are more relevant than heroes? Or could it be that society is simply not listening - even after all that has happened to its children? I mean, only someone who is psychologically deaf could come up with such a bizarre comment as, "*We in the Church have so much to offer* (the adult survivors of child sex abuse), *but they just won't listen to us!*

At this point I'm tempted to respond, "*The Church has nothing to offer such people*" but that would not be entirely true. The one and only thing that others can offer is what the abused have always looked for – a listening ear. It is the ear of someone who has the **humility** to acknowledge that he or she has been *less than heroic* in upholding the moral and ethical codes of the community, someone prepared to recognise that, when confronted by a hero, he or she is less worthy, and someone who can accept that their only stance before a living martyr - whose soul was murdered when upholding the moral standards of their community - is one of sheer and utter humility.

This being the case, it follows that you as an agent of that social world must look upon your adult clients, who had been sexually abused as children, with the utmost *humility*. Call it, "*Unconditional positive humility*" if you like. No other stance is necessary, and no other suffices. It is that simple because it is the truth.

Conclusion

We have come a long way in this chapter from the stomach of a hungry child, to the adolescent eye on morality and, finally, to the listening ear of the adult. On that journey I have highlighted three issues: the significance of *hope*, the requirement for a balance between *wisdom and heroism*, and ultimately the necessity for *humility* when listening to those who survived the incredible. It will take a certain wisdom and heroism for you to listen humbly and so bring hope to the child-like. Unfortunately, the virtues of wisdom, heroism and humility are alien in a social world only interested in 'winners'. Success in winning is all that matters, not how the game was played. The prize has become more important than the performance, and looking-good is now more relevant than looking back at how one acted. In short, the end now justifies the means.

It was this type of mentality that led Americans to hold ticker-tape parades for the heroes who won WW1 and WW2, but who refused to extend a similar welcome to those who had failed to win in Vietnam; as with the Korean War, that in Vietnam was destined to become another 'forgotten war'. The point being that soldiers in all these wars acted *heroically* whether they eventually won or not. If so, then clearly the parades were not to honour the heroism of the ordinary G.I. but to celebrate the feats of their commanders ('quarter-backs' in American Football) in winning the war.

The consequence for those Vietnam Veterans was appalling. Of the four million who fought so heroically, one million developed *Post Traumatic Stress Disorder* on returning home. This sobering fact led psychiatrists and psychologists to realise how important the attitude of society is for those who have been affected by either war or sexual abuse etc. If society turns its back on the survivors, the latter will experience great difficulty in recovering from psychological trauma. But if society surrounds the victims with visible support, their recovery will be much quicker. This is now a widely accepted conclusion.

However, the implementation of it in our society is

proving difficult. As I said, we are now more interested in the final outcome than the performance input. As a result, we tend to ignore those whom we view as losers. *"Why don't those people just go back to where they came from?"* is hardly a supportive response to immigrants – let alone to those who feel exiled inside their own country.

The truth of the matter is that *all children are immigrants*. All come into our world as strangers who have to be welcomed and nurtured, taught our customs and language, shown the community's codes of ethical and moral behaviour, listened to and, above all else, made to feel at home.

The more shocking truth is that many of us are abusing both immigrants and children; the same, *"What's in it for me?"* attitude lies behind both types of abuse. The same code of the abusive family, *"Don't wash your dirty linen in public!"* and call for secrecy, can be found in either scenario. The same tendency for the strong to take advantage of the weak can be found in every city, town, village and rural area across this land. Don't we all know this? Why, then, are we shocked when abuse is exposed? Could it be that we all **fear** that, someday, our own hidden and abusive behaviour will also be uncovered?

I believe the latter fear is behind our corporate response to abuse in any of its forms. If so, this may explain my reservations about certain adult survivors of child sexual abuse taking matters into the public forum; they are fostering an attitude of fear and anxiety in a society that is already full of it. They are exposing others to the terror that they once felt as children. By so doing, they are undermining that which they need the most – social support! No compensation will make up for that loss.

Such adults may argue, *"But we had no alternative other than litigation!"* If so, to this I reply, *"There is no such thing as 'no alternative'; there are only alternatives that have not been discovered as yet.*"

Again, lest anyone think I am opposed to such survivors of abuse let me add that it is only their tactics that I view as unwise. As with Rogers' counselling principles, what is useful in a private setting can be dangerous in a group or public forum – especially when those involved appear to know little about trauma and its effects, either on themselves or on others. As it stands, both the abused adults and society have locked themselves into focusing on child sex abuse. Perhaps if both changed their mutual positions to considering the possibility of trauma on either side, a better solution for all might be found. It may sound incredible, but it certainly is desirable.

8. THE THIRD PARADIGM

So far I've referred to the two paradigms out of which counsellors operate – that of Priest and of Wise One. I've also indicated that any counselling session which involves the theme of evil requires that you adopt the paradigm of Priest. Furthermore, that the session should be viewed in terms of a meeting, not of a relationship – and that it should be viewed as an impersonal meeting of two roles, not of two persons. Given, then, that you as counsellor play the role of Priest, what role does the client play? I hope to answer that question in this chapter. To do so, however, it is necessary to consider the stage on which the actors will carry out their roles.

1. The stage as real

Shakespeare, that most insightful of writers, coined the phrase, *"The thralles of sleepe"* (a 'thrall' being a slave) to describe those in taverns who drank to the point of falling asleep! Most of us on the other hand would probably refer to them as *thralls of alcohol,* reflecting our tendency to consider causes rather than results. The Bard, however, was closer to the truth in identifying *sleep* as the main issue, not the means used to reach such a state.

Sleeping is the major job of an infant – and also of those

who die; you spend your time in the womb and tomb asleep, but decrease the amount of time spent on it when awake. This led primitive people to make a distinction between the 'real world' and the 'dream world', a distinction that we make as well. But whereas we view the 'dream world' as that of sleep, and the 'real world' as that of the society in which we live by day, *they viewed them in reverse*. To them, the social world was a nightmare of constant terror, and only by escaping into sleep at night could one find relief from the terror; I say this because it is not possible to dream about a frightening 'absence' (which is what we mean by evil), only about a 'presence'. To be awake in the social world was, for them, to be in the 'dream world', while to be asleep at night was to be in the 'real world'. In short, their understanding of 'the real' and 'the dream' was back-to-front from ours.

This had both a religious and social consequence. Since their gods had created the 'real world' to begin with, then all their religious ceremonies were geared towards putting the congregation asleep! To that end, they used ritual activities and chants that acted as tranquillisers through their very monotony, working from the paradoxical premise that the best way to be present to the gods was to be absent from the demons of the secular world. In other words, entry into their 'real world' was only possible if all involved went into a *trance*. Furthermore, if the monotonous and hypnotic chanting and ritual dancing were insufficient to create the desired effect, one could always resort to drugs to enhance a religious state. *'Emptying the mind'* was not only their method of removing the terrible memories of what had happened to them when awake, but also the core requirement for finding the 'real world' of their religion. In both instances, the secret lay in escaping from the *'here and now'* of the present, and returning to the *'there and then'* of the past – just as it is for every traumatised client in counselling.

Something along those lines happened in the Korean Prison Camps. Many of the traumatised American POWs who had been cut-off from family, friends, officers and country took to their beds, curled up in the foetal position, and were found dead, usually three days later. In order to escape the nightmare world of their solitary existence, they turned to the 'real world' of sleep – and never came back.

But then, so do alcoholics and drug addicts. All become 'thralls of sleep' as being the only worthwhile reality; all want to be 'spaced out' in order to get back 'to the beginning' (birth). All engage in ritual behaviour involving a trance-like state. All seek to escape the same nightmare of their existence. In short, all are people on a spiritual quest - but knocking on the wrong doors.

In a similar way, the abused find that they too now live in a back-to-front world where they can't say what is 'real' or 'dream' anymore. While society views the original abuse as a nightmare and its caring response as real, the abused see society's reaction as their nightmare, and view what happened to them in the past as something real.

2. The stage as dream

It may be noticed that, originally, the above two stages - the real and the dream - were connected like Siamese Twins and, in effect, were one. With the passing of time, a separation took place. The first of these stages moved into the daytime, and is now referred to by us as *religion* properly speaking. But, while the second (the dream world of primitive man) remained in the daytime, it evolved, changed its name and became eventually known as *the social world* – hence all our references to the latter being no more than a dream or illusion, albeit a necessary one. If you like, religion represents humanity's eternal search for *reality*, while the social world functions as a temporary and illusory one since, *"I still haven't found what I'm looking for!"* Such a concept, of course, is entirely contradictory to the modern European belief that religion is all about illusion, while society *is* reality!

It is only when a human being is exposed to abuse in the form of either sex or violence at the hands of others, that the illusion of social consistency and permanence is wrecked. As indicated previously, the social world operates by developing myths that help its citizens remember the meaningful, the most significant being that *nothing changes,* and that we still do things 'the way we always did them'. Indeed, our very human values of faith, hope and love are entirely based on the *security* that society supplies when it assures us with the myth that nothing changes.

Shocking events, however, destroy the illusion that nothing changes and so bring down the entire house of cards built on hope and its accompanying fantasies. When this happens, our primary social values of faith and love collapse like houses in an earthquake, and are replaced by feelings of anxiety, guilt and depression; faith is replaced by anxiety, hope by depression and love by guilt as everything has now changed! In fact, all traumatised people will tell you, *"My whole life changed!"* after a shocking event.

From this it is easy to see what they require – some new form of security that will be comforting and consistent. This, of course, explains why they cry out for their mothers. It also gives you, the trauma counsellor, some idea of what you must supply – comfort and consistency in a secure environment. In other words, you have to speak soothingly so as to comfort, behave in a consistent manner so that they can trust again and, above all, ensure that they feel safe with you. *Safety for a traumatised person is a matter of life and death.* And the only way they can feel safe is to be in control of themselves and their environment – including you!

Naturally, this is when the power struggle occurs. They will want to control you, and you, of course, have to be in control of yourself. The only way you can keep some degree of control in such situations is *by giving them permission* to be in control – at least for as long as their anxiety is high. This means that you have to be prepared to go along with their desires – up to a point; if their desire would only lead to you being damaged, you have to draw a line. But ordinarily, most clients will only test your *willingness* to go along with them (I had more than one client who refused to let me look at them in the eye; either I ended up talking to them while gazing out of the nearby window, or they gazed out while talking to me!)

The curious thing is that the attacker came from the social stage, and often represented it to the child at the time. As a result, the alienated child seems to resort to the archaic and primitive forms of dealing with terror, namely, engaging in ritual behaviour while moving towards the trance-like condition of those involved in primitive religious ceremonies; in children this can take the form of rocking - a form of liturgical dance - or of acting-out the abuse in play form. Like their ancestral predecessors, they seek a ritual *purity* so as to restore a lost innocence and, to that end, move towards isolation in their search for *power.* Innocence and power go together according to Mircea Eliade; both are characteristics of God (and also of the new-born infant). And both are to be found 'at the beginning' of time; they are not to be found in the time that passes, but in the time that never flows (eternity). It may be for this reason that traumatised people seek to escape from the time known as 'now' and go back to that known as 'then' in their search for a lost innocence. They seek such an 'innocence' since in their hearts they believe that they are both contaminated by abuse *and evil in their person.*

Once you understand the secret 'religious' activities of

the abused, it makes a certain sense to support them in their efforts. To that end, some of us in the North of Ireland suggest to abused clients that they locate '*the centre of the world*' in their life – some garden or place that is '*special*' to them. There they are to dig a small hole in the ground with a view to planting a tree. But before they do so, they are to take the written version of their trauma story, burn it and place the ashes at the bottom of the hole. Only then do they plant the sapling on top of the ashes. Clearly, the message is that out of death will come life in the form of a mature tree. The latter will later serve as a memorial to 'what happened' that, in turn, releases the person from acting as the perpetual monument! "*I know that you'll never forget the past, but you don't have to go through life forever remembering it! The tree will do it for you.*"

As I said, we live and perform on two stages - just like primitive people - the 'real' and the 'dream'. Planting a tree in the above manner takes care of the latter, thus freeing the person to focus on the former – his or her own home, symbol of the *real*.

3. Home

One of the consequences of a traumatic experience is that the abused begin to feel like '*strangers in their own home*'. Psychiatrists and psychologists are aware of this, but few try to explain the phenomenon. Only religion has an explanation. To understand this, go back to what I said about primitive people wanting to live 'at the centre of the world, and at the beginning of time'. If you think about it, that centre is your original family home, and the beginning refers to your birth; one represents that 'special place' and the other that 'special time'. This explains why primitive people dealt with terror by *settling* themselves, that is to say, by re-creating their original home in a settlement. If so, you would be wise to learn and use the language of the construction industry – *building* and its associated terms ('foundation', 'rooms', 'doors', 'windows', 'corridors', 'fireplace and chimney', 'roofs' etc.). In other words, don't think of 'solving problems' but of helping clients to *rebuild* their lives, that is to say, to rebuild a shattered *world* and an equally devastated *home*. However, for all practical purposes, a 'world' and a 'home' are almost interchangeable terms. And perhaps it might be useful to begin with the latter since it will be easier to grasp.

3.1 Home and Safety

A home for most people is the place in which they feel both safe and loved. If so, it is true to say that you have four homes in this life: your body, your mother's womb, your house and your culture. In each of these you feel – or once felt – 'at home'. This explains why all traumas involve an attack on one or more of these homes; you become shocked, for instance, if anyone attacks your body, burglarises your house, practices abortion, or lifts you out of your culture and drops you into a completely different one. If so, it is true to say that *you can't have a trauma separate from a 'home' in one of the above four senses.* When you hear of 'trauma', think of 'home'.

In the case of the American POWs in Korea, their links with home were damaged by their captors who censored their in-coming mail; "Dear Son" letters – those that had been written in a loving way – were destroyed whereas, "Dear John" letters that had been written in a negative and scolding manner, were always delivered to the prisoners. As a consequence, those who received no mail were disappointed, but then so were those who received it! As a result, both began the process of losing interest in - and separating themselves from - those back home.

Implications

Given the significance of the term *home* to the traumatised, you prepare the counselling room so that it suggests a home. For example, you arrange the seating so that you and the client are sitting comfortably on either side of a fireplace (symbol of the mother), that there is a large clock (symbol of the father – as in 'father time') on the mantelpiece, and that the walls are decorated with pictures that describe something beautiful (and that would appeal to a young child). All the above are useful for 'setting the stage' upon which the drama will unfurl.

3.2 World

The 'world' is not the same thing as the earth or planet. Rather, the world is the *story* or myth you tell yourself and others to explain your history. To understand this, think of a spider; it takes something from within itself, spins a web and then lives at the centre of that web-world. Likewise, people 'spin a yarn' and live at the centre of their story-world. And since no two people tell the same story, then each lives in his or her separate world!

Trauma occurs when the delicate threads that hold their story-world together are suddenly severed; their 'whole world' goes to pieces, so to speak. Once broken, the threads cannot be pieced together again; a damaged world cannot be repaired, it can only be re-created – as every spider knows!

Again, in the case of the POWs, the Chinese at no time encouraged the prisoners to become Marxist. Rather, they encouraged them to read American newspapers that recorded all the 'bad news' from the States. They then asked the men what they were doing in Korea when, clearly their own country was in such a mess! They also encouraged them to read the writings of Charles Dickens, stories about how poor children in Western Society – like

Oliver Twist – had to cope with a brutal environment. The effect of all this 'bad news' on the POWs was to start the process of separating them from their own culture – as surely as the middle class in Northern Ireland has begun the process of separating itself from its culture by not voting after years of negative news. An overdose of bad news about 'the world' only makes people want to forget – as every traumatised person knows fully.

In summary, then, whenever a person experiences a trauma, their world comes to an end and, as a result, they no longer feel at home in either their family, society or culture.

4. The third paradigm

Previously, I've indicated that The Priest served as architect to the community in its attempts to create 'a better world'. I also noted that the maintenance and even enhancement of this 'better world' was the function of The Wise Ones in the form of Hero and Wise Woman. Clearly, these paradigms are not applicable to the traumatised whose 'worlds' and 'homes' have been obliterated by abuse. Some other paradigm is required.

Throughout this book, I have laid down a series of clues as to what that paradigm might be. And to a large extent, you as reader have to find the answer as do those who work on Su Doku – by a process of elimination! To begin with, this paradigm has to be impersonal (is not a person), and child-like in many ways (not part of a rational adult's view of the world). Secondly, it has something to do with religion rather than with psychiatry or psychology as such. Thirdly, it has something to do with that which can't be seen, heard or touched because it is somehow enclosed in a protective membrane. Fourthly, it is associated with night-time and sleep (not the daytime). Fifthly, it is 'enthralling' or a thrall of some sort. Sixthly, it is associated with 'the beginning and the end of the world', or has to do with the womb and the tomb (is asleep and not fully alive or awake) and has all the qualities of mystery! Finally, it is something you *meet with* rather than *relate to* in the dark.

The answer, of course, is The Ghost! In other words, the traumatised person **adopts the paradigm - or plays the part - of The Ghost on the social stage of life**. It is important that you grasp this concept since, clearly, such clients will play this role in your counselling room.

4.1 The Vanishing

There are several good reasons for their adopting this role, the main one being that they experience themselves as dead in spirit yet somehow living. Accordingly, they don't play the part of a dead man (which admirably describes the activity of the depressed) but rather that of a zombie-like being in a limbo between the living and the dead. As part of that role, they become invisible (*"I just want to disappear"*) and wish they could vanish altogether (*"I don't like people looking at me"*). They also tend to float or drift through life, moving as though deaf, dumb and blind to what is going on around them.

A classic illustration of this phenomenon occurred during the Nazi era in Europe; Jewish prisoners lined up like lambs before an open pit, while waiting their turn to be shot; they appeared to be oblivious of what was going on around them. Any sensible person, realising that they had nothing to lose, would have attacked their murderers and 'gone down fighting'. So why were those men so different? The answer, of course, is that they had already been traumatised and had gone into that sleep-like state of the living dead. If you like, they didn't walk as men to their deaths; rather, they sleep-walked as ghosts! Today, we clearly recognise that this semi-paralysed state is due to the body administering a merciful opiate to the system which numbs the person so that they feel no pain at the end. The same drug also fosters a sort of paralysis that inhibits movement (refer back to van der Kolk's observation that those who *can move* during a traumatic event recover from it fairly quickly, while those who can not take much longer), leaving the 'ghost' totally helpless to influence the world about.

4.2 The Helpless Untouchable

Acting from the paradigm of The Ghost isn't easy. It results in the traumatised losing interest in everything that once mattered to them in their former life.

I mean, if you are a ghost, why would you want to work and make some money? Why would you want to go to a party – unless, of course, you intended to get 'stoned out of your mind' and find some peace in sleep? Why plan anything when you have no future? How could you possibly benefit as a ghost from being told, *"You've got to pull yourself together and get on with your life!"* Why would you want to think of danger when you're no longer alive? Why would you as ghost want to study or grow? How could you possibly feel at home when your role requires that you haunt the house? How do you enjoy the opera when you're The Phantom? How do you sit down, put up your feet and relax when you are The Ghost-That-Walks? How do you love people when your job as a ghost is to scare them? How can you forgive those who 'murdered your soul' when, as the living dead, you are now in a separate world - the after-life - where the Law of Retribution has replaced the former Jubilee Law of Forgiveness? What good is compensation to you when you're dead?

As I said, playing the role of The Ghost is a difficult job, but one that many abused children consider when they say, *"I wish I was dead! That would show them!"* Playing the actual role of Ghost is easier for the adult, and for the same reason, *"That would show them!"*

4.3 The Explanation

The question may arise as to how a childish Halloween mask became a social role. The answer appears to lie in the coming together of two separate principles. The first is psychological: *the more terrifying the external event, the greater the allegiance to the group* – as everyone who has lived through the 'troubles' in Northern Ireland will know. (For those with a psychological background, 'allegiance to the group' is known as a transference – the total sum of projections; both allegiance to the group and transference are useful in the taming of terror).

The second and more sociological principle is: *the more terrifying the external oppressor, the greater the possessiveness of the oppressed.* In other words, oppressed minorities around the planet seek to possess the so-called power of the oppressor in an obsessive manner, that is to say, as if possessed by an evil spirit. Furthermore, devil worship and the need for exorcisms in society is a *religious* phenomenon that appears whenever that society is oppressed by a stronger external and *political* force - hence the paradox experienced in Iraq by Muslims when some of their people became possessed by diabolical tendencies (suicide bombers) even as they opposed the Great Satan of American military power. But then, the same thing happened to the oppressed communities in Northern Ireland; minorities appeared which likewise argued that the end justified the means – and that only diabolical means would remove the Great Satan (or 'evil presence' as it was known in Northern Ireland) from this island!

In short, it is this combination of *attachment to the group* to tame terror, together with the *obsession with power* to create terror that led to The Ghost becoming a social role; on the one hand, ghosts cling to the social world and, on the other hand, terrify it.

5. Attachment and Obsession

Adult victims of child sexual abuse play the role of The Ghost. On the one hand, they become overly attached to their abuser (society) while, on the other hand, showing that same society what it has done to them. Their abuse leaves them thinking, *"I wish I was dead!"* while their later transformation into The Ghost leaves them thinking, *"That will show them what they've done to me!"*

Since they lack the vocabulary to 'utter the unutterable', they play-act 'what happened' so that others can experience the mystery (the abuse which they recall as pictures in their memory). Only by *showing* the mystery, can they learn its consequences - the *terror* that they want others to see and put into words since they can't; they don't know they're terrified since they lack the words to describe the state they're in, *"Words can't express what I've been through!"*

If you think about it, *"That will show them what they've done to me"* simply means, **"Will someone please show me what society has done to me since I haven't got the slightest idea!"**

Given the importance of attachment and obsession, I now want to consider both separately.

5.1 Attachment

In order to tame terror, the child instinctively clings to its family and to society as I shall say more about in the next chapter. In essence, this clinging amounts to the child becoming the *shadow* of the social world. If you think about it, your shadow is outside of yourself but goes wherever you go. It may vanish in the dark but appears *whenever you turn your back to the light*, or when you live in a back-to-front world. In a similar manner, the abused child becomes attached to society and becomes its shadow –

or ghost. Like a shadow, the ghost is something attached to and *created by the social world itself.* It is something that won't go away, something clinging that is 'as one' with society, something forever attempting to vanish into society for safety. In short, something in FLIGHT. As an abused client once told me, *"Fear gave me wings!"*

5.2 Obsession

Besides clinging to society to tame its terror, the child also becomes obsessed with his or her own innocence. That's because all abused children sincerely believe that they magically *caused* the adult to do what he did, and that they are to blame for 'what happened'; they believe they are not innocent.

However, as already mentioned, innocence and power are almost interchangeable terms, according to Eliade, in that both are characteristic of the gods; the all-powerful are innocent, and the innocent are all-powerful. In other words, any movement towards power or empowerment is a movement towards innocence. And to lose innocence is to lose power; it is to be *helpless* in this world. This explains the subsequent *obsession with power* in the abused; they want to restore a lost innocence. All abused adults become obsessed with power, authority and control; all become ghosts (as did Adolf Hitler who was also abused as a child) obsessed with proving their innocence and determined to prove that some other party was guilty. In reality, what they are attempting to show is that they as adults are innocent, but as children were guilty. In short, they are haunted by terrifying memories of childhood, and currently seek power to FIGHT their terror of the divine Nemesis - the child they used to be!

In summary, then, The Ghost is both the *shadow of the social world,* and *the shade of a long-gone child.* It is attached to both society-as-good to tame terror, and to child-as-bad to create terror. It engages in flight and fight; it disappears, and appears. In short, it alternates between two extremes – *All* and *Nothing*, with the former term meaning 'God', and the latter term meaning, 'Satan'.

As I have consistently indicated in this book, trauma is essentially a religious phenomenon with human consequences.

5.3 Implications

I need to repeat that abused adults have no awareness of their having *become* The Ghost that once was part of an original childish game of 'pretend'. Nor are they aware that The Ghost is a universal *religious* response to the abuse of *political-social* power, a response that tries to show something to the rest of the world of what's going on at home, namely, that 'souls are being murdered' by the abuse of power. If you like, the appearance of The Ghost of Halloween is a child's cry for help; it implies that the child has been 'tricked' when 'treated' by a predator from the social world.

It is the job of the trauma counsellor to recognise that cry for help, and to point out to the client that there is a better way of playing the role of The Ghost.

In the Christian tradition, the Ghost of Halloween is but a childish parody on the real and adult Ghost of Pentecost (The Holy Ghost). In other words, the true role of The Ghost is 'to show' something to the living (that's why Shakespeare had the ghost of Hamlet's father appear to him, and why Dickens had ghosts appear to Scrooge).

The Ghost's role is to create a display, to make an exhibition of itself in order that it may be looked at. Its job is to put a light where it can be seen as a signal, to point out the way in the dark, to reveal the inner beauty that was destroyed by the ugliness of evil, to show that goodness will always prevail over evil, and to show that there is life after death. In cases of child sex abuse, the role of The Ghost is *to show society the good the child has done for it,* not just the damage that society and its agents caused to the child. The Ghost invariably focuses on the light (which is why it appears as white), not the darkness. Accordingly, the true role of the abused as Ghosts is to cast a little light on the darkness of others in the social world. As the President said in the movie, *Independence Day*, "We will not go silently into the night!" Likewise, the abused must be discouraged from remaining invisible and mute beings, but rather encouraged to 'show' themselves for what they really are – beautiful people who surround themselves with things of beauty and life. It is always better to 'light a candle than to curse the darkness'.

6. Therapeutic response

Psychiatrists who study the effect of the *body* on the mind have for some time been using the religious term, *The Ghost*, to describe the sexually abused. But, as mentioned previously, they've also noticed how such people speak in religious terms when describing their experiences as a *'living hell'*. Psychiatry comes close to religion.

On the other hand psychologists who study the effect of the *group* on the mind have shown less evidence of any interest in the concept of *Ghost*. Their concern has mostly been in getting the traumatised safely back into society. And if changing the thinking of the abused works to that end, so much the better for society – which can carry on with its regular life as if nothing had happened. (Aaron Beck, the psychiatrist, with his 'quick-fix' Cognitive Behavioural Therapy appears to have the same goal in mind).

The ethics behind such 'brainwashing' of the individual for the common good is debatable. Does the end really justify the means? There is, of course, no doubt that the abused benefit from such training (although it must be said that there appears to be little evidence about its long-term effects). Of greater concern, however, is that all such therapies appear to effectively prevent the abused from carrying out their role as The Ghost. As a result, society merrily continues as it always has – without having learned a single thing about abuse, and without feeling the need to examine and change itself in any way.

From the above it should be clear that you, the trauma counsellor as Priest, meet the client as Ghost, not so much to 'show' something to them, but to allow them to 'show something to you'. To that end, the client puts on a series of masks, apparently in the mistaken belief that the play is about Halloween; the mask of Wicked Witch (derived originally from 'Weak or Weaked Victim') is very popular. So also is the mask of Monster etc.

Your mission is, as I said, to help them recognise that *they actually **are terrified***, and that they are now playing the part of Ghost. Furthermore, that the play is about Pentecost, not Halloween. If so, tell them that the proper way to appear or exhibit as Ghost is to become a 'candle in the wind', a flame of love casting light into the darkness of others; it is to *move* lightly through the night so as to reveal the inner *beauty* of the soul that once was murdered. In short, you speak in the childish form of metaphor, simile and analogy with which the child-like can identify.

You also talk in the language of the fairytale, *"As the rose in winter does not die but only goes asleep while protected by surrounding briars, so the Sleeping Beauty never died but went asleep for one hundred years in a Castle surrounded by briars. You too are now asleep but will waken when ready to do so. Till then, you play the part of The Ghost or Spirit of the child that once was 'thralled by sleepe'. Perhaps it would help if you became your own Prince Charming!"*

By bringing such unconscious and beautiful forms to the

client's awareness, you empower her since, gradually, she realises that *she can make a choice* – to keep on sleeping as a restless Ghost, or to waken to love and life. When she wakens to that reality, your task is then to help her find an alternative role in society.

7. Alternative roles

Those alternative roles are that of 'Hero' or 'Wise Woman'. Neither of these paradigms will initially be acceptable to your client. Thinking as they do as children, they will be convinced that they *caused* the villain to act as he did; *"I know, 'cause I was there!"* So begins the power-struggle that I mentioned earlier. While they try to convince you of their 'evil', your task is to tell them the truth, namely, that what the predator did was evil, but that they as children at the time *upheld the moral standards of the community by being obedient in an extraordinary circumstance,* and that by doing so *they were very wise at the time.* In other words, you encourage the adult survivor of child sex abuse to accept the unacceptable, namely, that they have always been heroic and wise but just didn't know it!

I call this truth 'unacceptable' for the simple reason that *society does not accept it as the truth.* Rather, it prefers to label its abused children with the demeaning title of 'victim'. But notice how nations award their physically wounded war veterans with medals (such as The Purple Heart in the U.S.) and never refer to them as 'victims'. If so, one can only wonder why no medals are awarded to women and children who have been wounded both physically and mentally by abuse *while upholding the moral standards of that same society.* Surely such *heroism and wisdom* merits a similar form of acknowledgement by society.

As it stands, society appears more interested in banishing its 'victims' to another world (as in the Irish legend of *'The Children of Lir'* where the white ghosts on the lake of silence were called *swans*, and where no Christian bell would ring for a thousand years to awaken them from their sleep).

Till such bells start ringing, it is of the utmost importance that you begin the process of praising such 'victims' for their bravery, courage and wisdom, not to bolster their ego, but simply because it is the truth. And as I said earlier, it takes a lot of *humility* to acknowledge the truth – both on the part of the counsellor and of the client.

Conclusion

You will have noticed in this chapter that I have focused on paradigms. This may be a little frustrating for those who would have preferred if I had said more about behaviour, on the assumption that outcomes are determined by actions, not wishful thinking. Such, of course, is the primary interest of an ordinary counsellor.

However, as indicated previously, the key issue for the sexually abused, alcoholics etc is not morality but religion. The issue is not 'what to do' but, rather, **'who am I?'** or else **'what value do I have**?' – especially in a situation where the predator once damaged *a person* in the form of a child, and where the society from which that predator came refuses to accept the testimony of the abused.

Given that boys abused by men can suffer *an identity* problem, and that girls suffer a *loss of worth* (dignity or 'beauty'), it follows that both find themselves cut-off from the social world (your identity is determined to a large extent by how society *sees* you, your worth by what society is *looking* from you; if not seen or looked at, you begin to vanish, become invisible and, finally, see and look upon yourself as a Ghost). In turn, to be outside of the social world is, in effect, to be *'an outlaw forever hunted by the posse'*, *'a scout riding ahead of the prairie wagons'* (these images of 'fringe people' are used by American theorists to describe the loneliness of '*the ghost-riders in the sky*', of the abused in their relationship with the social world).

To be on the fringe in the above manner is to be in a world that is back-to-front to the extent that the abused person no longer knows what is 'real' or 'dream'. It is the experience of living in a topsy-turvy world that leaves the person thinking that everything they once thought was 'good' is now 'bad', where living a lie is considered better than telling the truth, where black is actually white and so on. Not surprisingly, most begin to think they are going crazy! In short, their greatest problem lies not in dealing with an abuser in the past, nor just in dealing with the physical symptoms of trauma in the present but, rather, in *dealing with a shocked society* at all times!

Essentially, that problem lies in the social tendency to view the disgrace of others as one's own. The result for society is **shame**; it becomes ashamed on learning what some of its members did to children. And it is this very painful shame that is conveyed to the abused who, in turn, begin to see themselves as the source of it all in the first instance – hence their tendency to hide. In other words, those who were sexually abused as children learn from an ashamed society the meaning of *shame.*

If so, there would seem to be a connection between the recovery of society and that of the abused. The sooner society recovers from its shock, stops feeling so ashamed and begins to welcome its heroes and wise women, the better for all concerned. In short, the sooner all focus on religion and 'being' rather than on morality and 'doing', the quicker will be the recovery of all concerned.

For this reason, I focused on paradigms rather than on behaviour. Paradigms, roles or models refer to a person's *being and becoming*; they are useful in establishing an identity that society can both recognise and value.

Accordingly, you would be wise to limit your in-put to observations about the client's courage and wisdom, rather than referring directly to your client's specific activities as such. By all means encourage her to play the role, but be careful about commenting too much on how she carries it out. Trust her judgement in the execution, but make sure her actions are in keeping with the paradigm.

For example, while it is all right for her to say quite a bit about her past to those who need to know (such as social workers, police etc), it is not all right to do so with others. In a small group of family and friends, she may acknowledge that she had been sexually abused without going into any details, but when dealing with the general public *she must never use the terms, 'sexual abuse',* since the public do not need to know.

Instead, she only admits in a public forum (to employers, business associates etc) that she had been *'traumatised when younger'* without going into any further detail. And if pushed to elaborate, her response should be, *"It had to do with violence but I don't want to talk about it."* This type of response is so vague that it will leave the listener wondering what sort of violence – but that is really none of their business. In short, while it may be heroic to talk, it is wise for the abused to say as little as possible about evil to a public that thinks like a child as a general rule.

In summary, then, begin by encouraging the client to focus on her five senses and her body so that she can become 'grounded' rather than floating through life as a Ghost, then move to those paradigms which will help her relate with society in a more realistic way – those of the Hero and The Wise Woman. In short, start with 'the body' and end up with 'the society'.

9. LIBERATION

In the previous chapter, I ended by noting that the movement in the drama between trauma counsellor and client is from 'the body' of the individual to 'the social'; it is a movement from the particular to the universal. To say this is to repeat a theme that has appeared consistently throughout this book. For example, it is the psychological movement from childhood to adulthood. It is even the spiritual movement from magic to religion. Ultimately, it is about the means of finding a desirable happiness if not in this life, at least in a later one. For children, this 'later one' refers to the day when they grow up. For religious adults, it refers to another and different life. Any way you look at it, some form of evolution or development takes place in everyone's life.

What form of development, then, can there be for a Ghost 'enthralled by sleep'? The answer, as I hope to show, is to be found in the movement from personal slavery to social liberty. I shall begin by looking at how the abused become enchained in the first place.

1. Trust

Like hope, trust has its roots in breast-feeding. But whereas hope springs from the results of such feeding (*success* and *fulfilment*), trust refers more to the act of resting in the arms of the mother while being fed – hence its association with terms like *reliance, dependence and assurance*. And if hope is the foundation of a later confidence and love, then trust is the link between hope and confidence; it can refer to either. It goes without saying that if hope is damaged, so too is trust.

For our purposes, trust refers to the extent you are willing to be *vulnerable* in relation to another. If so, then it is possible to speak about levels of vulnerability. Those levels, in turn depend upon two variables: your ability to surrender control and, secondly, the consistency of the other.

1.1 Surrender Control

At the minimum, a component of trust is the giving of a right to another based on your ability to make a secure prediction about them. This is equivalent to extending your open right hand as a greeting. At a higher level, trust is a measure of the extent to which you are willing to put yourself in the hands of another. The more you do this, the more control is surrendered, the greater the risk and the more vulnerable you become. And, of course, the maximum level of such yielding is associated with love.

1.2 Consistency

The second variable is the *consistency* of the other. Again, the term consistency came from breast-feeding; it referred originally to the infant remaining at rest, later to the firmness and harmony of conduct whereby the mother enabled the child to sleep; the more consistent the former, the greater the level of trust in the latter.

In other words, where the other is inconsistent, or where your environment is ambiguous and forever changing, then your level of anxiety will increase in anticipation of not being satisfied, or of losing something in the future. In short, *you will not be able to trust or rest*. This holds true for the baby with its mother and for you in your environment.

2. Vulnerability

Trust is not normally much of an issue for you as a counsellor; you have been trained to put your trust in a new client, and to hope that, in time, the client will be able to trust you. It is, however, a greater issue for a client who is unwilling to admit *vulnerability*, and who then proceeds to resist all your efforts to 'help' them. Such resistance is useful; it enables you to identify those areas in which the client feels the greatest anxiety, and the most oppressed.

Secondly, trust for both you and your client is measured by your mutual ability to assess each other's level of consistency. When satisfied, both of you work on the assumption that the outcome will somehow be favourable, and soon settle down to begin the process of relating with each other.

Matters, however, become complicated when working with a traumatised client. For one thing, the latter can't possibly imagine any future outcome that will be favourable; their imagination is impaired. Secondly, they as Ghost simply have no sense of *vulnerability*; that's because they are entirely blind to danger and, in any case, dead people can't feel 'hurt', 'vulnerable' or any of the other inappropriate terms used by an equally blind society to describe someone whose soul has been murdered.

Thirdly, trust implies a willingness to surrender control, as noted previously. This, of course, is impossible for someone who once surrendered control as a child to an abusive adult, who is now a rest-less ghost, whose motto is now, "*Never again!*" and whose sanity requires them to stay in control of themselves and of their environment.

For an abused person, trusting the social world is not an issue. That's because it simply does not exist – anymore than does hope in it. For society to expect that an untreated abused person will eventually trust it, given enough time, is like waiting for the return of Adolf Hitler; it just won't happen.

This explains why it makes no sense for you to approach the abused hoping for a relationship based on mutual trust. It won't happen. Rather, it makes more sense to have a *meeting* with them – just as politicians still do business with those they don't trust; they know they are taking a gamble, and so try to reduce in advance the chance of loss as much as possible.

When I say that untreated adults who once experienced child sex abuse cannot trust the social world, this is not an accusation, nor a sign of malevolence, nor is it even a weakness. It is just a fact. Furthermore, it is true to say that such adults *have the right not to trust that world*.

3. Intimacy and Authority

Since the abused do not trust the social world, the question arises as to what they do as an alternative. Given that trust is the willingness to put yourself in another's arms, the answer to the question is fairly simple: the abused put a grip on the other's arms and won't let go. Such clinging, gripping or locking-on to the social world is characteristic of the behaviour of the abused. I call it the 'death grip', one not unlike that used by drowning people when approached by a would-be rescuer; it is a fierce, desperate attempt to hold on to life at any cost. It is entirely instinctive and not very reasonable. It is also dangerous for the rescuer.

This may explain what I said earlier that, *"Evil attaches"*; it is like a dark hole of emptiness that sucks everything into it. Sometimes the abused refer to it as, *"The abyss"*; they do not call it 'the pit' (which at least has sides even if no bottom) but some form of emptiness and nothingness that has neither sides, top nor bottom. To avoid such a disaster, the abused frantically seize anything within their reach – whether it is good for them or not, or whether it is useful or not. For them it is better to grab something than to grab nothing since life is a matter of *all or nothing*. This explains why, when they become attached to someone or something, letting go is not an option. It is this 'death grip', this inability to let go of something that creates the impression that the person is now extremely *restless, possessive* and *obsessive*. Call him or her a 'spoilt child', if you like – as long as you keep in mind who did the spoiling.

Effect on Intimacy

The combination of 'death grip' and inability to let go wreaks havoc with *intimacy* for the adult victim. Intimacy is closely associated with trust in that both involve a 'willingness to put yourself in another's arms'. Both involve a yielding, a resting and a surrendering to another; trust, intimacy and sexuality are inseparable from tenderness and vulnerability.

Unfortunately for the abused, they are not. Living as they do in a back-to-front world, they see no connection between intimacy and tenderness or vulnerability. Rather, intimacy is viewed more as a tryst (the appointed station in hunting) than a trust; it conjures up images of game to be pursued in a hunt. The goal in this distorted view of intimacy is to win or possess the heart of the chosen one (victim). Those interested in winning do not view their surrendering or resting as an option. They do not 'fall' in love but prefer to 'make' love to one of their possessions (*"You are all mine!"*) In short, for them, intimacy is to be pursued as part of the good life, not something that can be trusted to follow from a good relationship.

Effect on Authority

Precisely the same result appears when the abused put a 'death grip' on authority and will not let go. Authority is a major issue for groups who have to make a decision; the authority of the group is vested in one person who ultimately has to make that decision on behalf of the group as its representative. For this to happen, the other members of the group have to yield or surrender their individual opinions to that of the group. In short, they 'rest on their oars' while submitting to the group's authority.

Again, this simply is not possible for the abused who have to keep control in order to feel safe. Many leave, but some remain attracted by the impersonality and anonymity of groups. Some even become the group leader in their search for power and its accompanying solitude. From such a position, they then become quite possessive of all beneath them in the system and, as a result, are often considered abusive by their subordinates because they appear to be holding everyone in an iron grip ('death grip') as, for example, did Hitler. In short, such leaders cannot possibly trust their subordinates who, in turn, stop trusting their leader. For both parties, talking to the other is like *'talking to a brick wall!'* Accordingly, both go through life *'living lives of quiet desperation'*. It is hardly surprising if some such leaders of groups turn to suicide - be it personal, alcoholic, economic or political etc - as a way of finding rest and relief. Rather than let go of the social world, they prefer to let themselves go.

4. Addiction

This tendency of the abused to put a 'death grip' on someone or something, together with the refusal to let go is descriptive of an addict. Rather than submit to authority or to intimacy, the addict engages in a passive and narcissistic regression, a pseudo-form of rest. That, of course, is precisely what untreated victims of child sex abuse do; as ghosts they become as helpless and passive as were those Jewish prisoners in the concentration camps of World War 2 as already noted; the hunted become the haunted.

This 'return to childhood' results in the loss of any sense of boundaries, or to the loss of any sense of managing one's own body. It represents a final, desperate effort to fight total annihilation at the hands of an overpowering predator intent upon destroying their will.

It also leaves the 'victim' forever trying to figure out **WHY** their abuser did what he did rather than focusing on **HOW** to deal with the consequences of an attack; the former question is one that all children ask about the world; it reflects their curiosity about *causes* (about the person responsible for starting something) whereas the 'how' question is associated with adults more interested in the *end results* of impersonal social or environmental factors involved.

It is the '**Why**' question that leads the traumatised adult into becoming passive before an overwhelming environment; it is the question that leads to addiction rather than to devotion.

Addiction to Trauma

Most of the time, traumatised people feel under-aroused, depressed and empty. However, since trauma floods the body with a variety of adrenaline-based chemicals, it should be no surprise if they become physiologically and psychologically addicted to trauma.

Examples of such an addiction can be seen in the movies, *Fearless*, *The Pawnbroker*, the Russian roulette scene in *The Deer Hunter*, and the opening scene of *Apocalypse Now*.

Just remembering - or reliving - the original abuse can

give the person a 'high'. It can equally foster an addiction to drugs, alcohol, politics, religion, shopping and eating etc; in short, to any obsession which distracts them from what is important.

In all cases, the 'death grip' results in the person developing a fixation; they become 'locked in the service of a hopeless cause'. To the abused what is important is, not the hopelessness of a past cause, but their current fixated stance. After all, it is better to be fixed to something than to nothing! It is better to hang on than to rest.

Addiction to the Social World

What is important for survival to the abused is 'togetherness'. To that end they can become addicted to love; as mentioned previously, they pursue love and intimacy with intense feelings and a fierce hunger for unity. And, in their attempts to become *one* with the other, they pursue and hold on to such an extent that they lose their own individuality in the process; in this sense they are like a drowning man in the Artic who seizes hold of an iceberg for safety – and ends up frozen himself! An addictive attachment is one in which *the ability* ***to remain apart*** *from a social role is missing*.

Addiction to a Lost Innocence

For the same reason, alcoholics oppose authority. Instead of submitting to an outside authority, they engage in the passivity of a child. As a result they find themselves controlled by an internal power greater than that of the external one they've opposed.

Accordingly, it is true to say that an alcoholic doesn't *have* an addiction; he *is* the addiction! He and it have become as one. For him to 'let go' of his addiction would amount to letting go of his identity and worth; it would be to vanish into the nightmare of the abyss – the emptiness of an 'absence' or of a lost innocence or power. For him, it is better to be gripped by alcohol than by nothing.

5. Identifying symbols

It has been my experience that the abused identify with *a thing* that symbolises the original source, rather than with a *person* as such. Such things are related to one or more of the five senses – an object, a sound, a smell, a taste etc. that later in life act as 'triggers' in bringing it all back to life, so to speak.

Sometimes this symbolic thing appears in the form of a phobia. For example, on one occasion I met a female client who had developed a fear of going near children in case she touched them sexually. The very thought of doing so put her into such a state of panic that she was unable to go near children when working. It took some time to learn that she as a child had been severely burned in a fire. This led to her unwitting identification with the fire; *she and the fire had become as one*. This explained her terror of touching a child (lest it be burned). And the explanation as to why the phobia concerned sex was that the common denominator between fire and sex is *heat*. In short, she had identified with the fire, not with the neglectful parent who had briefly left her unsupervised in the room at the time; the thing had taken on symbolic meaning, the person had not.

Another example is that of a thirty-year old man who came for counselling because of his phobia about public toilets; he noticed that, when using a urinal and if approached from behind by another male, his system appeared to 'freeze'; he simply couldn't urinate – even though his bladder was full. In the last century such phenomena would have been attributed to a neurotic condition. Today, the trauma model explains it as a physiological reaction by the traumatised body to a trigger (in this case, the *sound* of an approaching footstep). If so, the initial trauma led to the ultimate freezing, and the shame became the consequent, not the antecedent. And, sure enough, the man in question turned out to have been sexually abused as a child by a male. Equally, his subsequent shame at being unable to function like other men led to his avoiding public toilets – and all events associated with them e.g. sports fixtures, theatres, bars etc. Ultimately, it led to him adopting a lonely lifestyle that, in turn, resulted in his being viewed by others as 'a bit anti-social', and 'a bit of a loner'. In this case, the 'thing' was the *sound* of a man's footsteps that had taken on symbolic meaning, not the 'person' of the man himself.

I call all these 'things' *symbols* because they - like all symbols - point to something other than themselves. In cases of abuse, that 'something' is the evil associated with the original abuser. This being the case, then all attempts by abused adults to ascribe their terror to a touch, sound, odour, taste, colour or object in view is nothing other than a childish attempt to create a symbol for evil.

Part of your work as a trauma counsellor is to point out to your client that the things which terrify them are only symbols, but that all point to the abusive person who set everything in motion from the very start. Pinning down that original source of all subsequent chaos in the life of the abused is important; if nothing else, it stops them from identifying *everyone* as the abuser! In short, it puts 'things' in perspective.

6. Letting go

There's the old story of the man who, on falling over a cliff, caught hold of a small tree growing out of the rock-face. In desperation, he cried out for help. The voice of God was heard from above, directing him to let go of the branch with his left hand. The man did so. The voice then directed him to let go with his right hand. At that point the man cried out, *"Is there anyone else up there?"*

Letting go of something upon which your life depends amounts to letting go of life. That's why those whose trust has been destroyed by abuse use a 'death grip' as though their life depended on it – which it does; as I said, it is better to hold on to something than to fall into The Abyss.

Or is it? I mean, what is so awful about an abyss? Come to think of it, what is an abyss other than nothingness? And why is it that people are afraid of nothing? Could it be that their greatest fear is of *being* a nothing, and that falling into it amounts to yielding to *oneself*? The latter, of course, is what we mean by addiction as previously mentioned in this chapter, hence the paradox of holding on addictively to avoid falling into addiction! You're damned if you hold on, and damned if you let go. In short, you are in a no-win situation where there are no other alternatives and where 'things' look hopeless.

But as I said in chapter 7, *"There is no such thing as 'no alternative'; there are only alternatives that have not been discovered as yet"*. And that undiscovered alternative lies in religion, not in psychology (as Carl Jung once pointed out to the future founders of Alcoholics Anonymous). Perhaps 'resting' consists in turning to 'The Higher Power' as the undiscovered alternative that can stop the desperate from 'falling into themselves'.

Surrendering

Counsellors and psychologists encourage clients to stand on their own two feet, take control of the situation, and so find happiness in their lives. Like Americans, everyone now seems to believe in, *"Life, liberty and the pursuit of happiness"* – for oneself, of course. And all these goals are to be pursued with restless zeal in a world that never sleeps.

By contrast, religion maintains that the only way to find happiness is to let go of it for oneself, and strive to bring happiness into the lives of others. To find authority, intimacy and life itself, you first must let go of all three, and allow them to come to you as something to be discovered, not pursued. It is this resting, letting go, yielding and surrendering to God and reality that a restless humanity finds so difficult to do.

Letting go of chains

In the case of adults who had been sexually abused as children, letting go amounts to liberating their abusers. After all, the principle, *"Evil attaches"* works two ways; the abuser is as much attached to the abused as the latter is to the former. As Afro- Americans used to say, *"You may have put a chain around me, but I am now the monkey on your back; wherever you go, I go. So, who's chained to whom?"*

Letting go means breaking the chains that enslave. It means recognizing that the abuser once broke the bonds that attached children to their families, and replaced them with chains that bound the children to him and to the social world. By breaking those chains and releasing the abuser and his society, the adult survivor will be liberated from both.

The abuser may once have had the power to initiate the meeting, but the abused now have the power to end it. This is why the words, *"It is over!"* have so much meaning to them. The 'thing' or 'meeting' is finally over – once the abused say it is! For the abused to realise this is to be empowered.

God once implied that *"It is over!"* when He liberated His people from slavery. As a consequence, no Hebrew back then was allowed to keep slaves indefinitely; after a certain length of time, all had to be released – whether the debts that had brought them into slavery in the first place had been repaid or not. Likewise, only The Ghost can liberate society from its slavery by determining when 'it is over'. The process of letting such slaves go and releasing them from their debts was - and still is - referred to as *forgiveness*.

7. Forgiveness

You need to know the above since both you and your client may confuse 'forgiving' with 'pardoning' or 'condoning'. A superior being (such as royalty) pardons as an act of mercy or generosity to those who have offended in serious matters, whereas condoning is based on pretence, *"Let's pretend it never happened!"*

To understand forgiveness, consider the wife of an alcoholic husband; she thinks that there are only two ways of dealing with him – put up with his nonsense or else throw him out through divorce. There is, of course, an alternative as I have stressed before in this book. This is called the *Third Way* by those who work with alcoholics.

The Third Way

For all practical purposes, the wife lets go of the alcoholic and gives him permission to solve his own problems. Before that can happen, she must first recognise her own addiction, that of helping him. She has to see how her addiction to helping is feeding his addiction to drinking; I mean, why should he help himself when someone else is already doing it for him? Paradoxically, to break her addiction, she has to let go of his addiction (or let go of *him* – since he and his addiction are one!)

In other words, in an emergency situation, the cardinal rule of survival is that you will first 'care for' yourself; *"Put the oxygen mask over your own face before putting it over your child's"* as they say on air flights. This means that, for the wife of an alcoholic, *everything she does must be done for herself.* For instance, if she puts her husband in hospital, it is not so that he will get better, but so that *she will get better.* By first caring for herself, she becomes liberated to *care about* - but not *care for* - him. In this way, she models what the alcoholic husband has to do - care for oneself!

This means that the wife has to learn what it means to be helpless before a disease like alcoholism. Instead of acting as if she was The Higher Power who is going to save her husband, she accepts her own helplessness and asks The Higher Power to help her – not him! In this way she learns what forgiveness really means – let him go or release him from her grip. Let him be the way he is. If anything, she has to protect herself from his disease.

In much the same way the adult survivor of child sex abuse has to learn this Third Way – that of separating themselves from their abuser and his addiction. The abused, of course, will say, *"You mean there's nothing I can do but let him go!"* just as the wife of an alcoholic will say, *"You mean there's nothing I can do but let him die!"* In both cases the answer is the same, *"Whether he lives or dies is not the issue. What is important is whether you live or die!"* If you want to live, let him go and let go of his addictive chains!

In other words, the whole purpose in the client forgiving an abuser is so that the former can liberate themselves from their **resentment**. That's what forgiveness means. It most certainly does not mean that the client absolves the abuser from his sins, nor condones anything he once did. It simply means, *"You are free to go. You owe me nothing. As far as I'm concerned, the past is history."* If you think about it, this amounts to saying, *"I bear you no grudge, nor want anything from you."* To forgive makes good sense since those who bear grudges, nurse resentment and go through life refusing to forgive only become depressed in the long term (as they turn into the darkness that they curse).

The Right Not to Forgive

The main point to keep in mind, however, when working

with a client is that *the abused have the right not to forgive.*
Although, if you think about it, this means that they have
the right to be the way they are as traumatised individuals.
If so, asking them to forgive their abuser is like asking
them to surrender their rights. And at that point the
question can arise once again: what is the best policy to
adopt - exercise a right or surrender it?

My view is that the upholding of the client's right is
necessary in the early stages of therapy, and the
surrendering of it advisable in the final stage. Between
these extremes, I rarely speak about forgiveness as such.
Rather, I focus on terms that are associated with it, such as
'acting impersonally', 'putting distance between yourself
and evil', 'separating from evil,' 'breaking addictive
attachments'. Later, I focus more on the need to 'trust', 'let
things go', 'loosen your grip on yourself'. In other words, I
want the client to move from playing the impersonal and
unforgiving Ghost to playing the impersonal but now
forgiving Ghost. The transformation is from a state of
constant motion and restlessness to one of inner stillness
and peace; it is not a change of role as such. The Ghost,
after all, is a symbol of the living, not of the dead. Its role is
to point to life after death, and only forgiving ghosts rest in
peace.

Having said that, I view even the act of forgiving by the
client as further evidence of their heroism and wisdom –
and have no hesitation in drawing this to their attention as
another sign that they should seriously think about
changing their role from Ghost to Hero and Wise Woman.
When they are ready to do so, of course.

Conclusion

Perhaps the most significant point to note in this chapter
is the difference between psychology and religion; the
former focuses on how to empower by taking control, the

latter on how to let go of power and control in order to find intimacy. The former focuses on how to keep danger out, the latter on letting wisdom in.

To understand this, it is useful to recognise the connection between these themes of power and intimacy in a group setting. All groups - be they religious or otherwise - discover that any movement towards intimacy and togetherness is dependent upon a successful resolution of the power struggle that precedes it. In a sense it is true to say that the movement towards intimacy is not unlike that towards birth; both are preceded by a painful struggle! This means that the antecedent power struggle leads to pain, and that the latter appears to be nature's way of ensuring a consequent attachment. As I said, *"Evil attaches!"*

In other words, and in a group setting, the restless power struggle surrounding authority precedes the restful resolution that leads to intimacy; the question, *"Which of us is the boss?"* precedes that of, *"How close will I get to you?"* This means that, of the two issues, authority and intimacy, the former is the more primitive. This is as true for couples in a relationship as it is for board members at a meeting. It is as true for counsellors as it is for trauma counsellors.

Only hopeless romantics and idealists like Carl Rogers believe that it is possible to find intimacy without authority, to find knowledge without reading - that is to say, without submitting to the authority of an author - or to find love without pain. The truth of the matter would seem to be that we first learn what *submission* means by dealing with authority. Once we've learned how to *submit to power*, we are better prepared - and in a better position - to *submit to love* and, as a result, find intimacy later. If, on the other hand, we view power as something to be pursued, seized, grabbed, or run away from, then later we will tend to view love and intimacy in precisely the same terms.

If so, it follows that disturbances associated with

authority will appear later as disturbances associated with intimacy – as all sexually abused children know full well. The sexual abuse of an individual child *is always preceded by a social abuse of power by authority*; the former abuse only points to the latter. If you like, 'authority' and 'intimacy' are not two entirely distinct entities; both form a continuum as in a magnet, with authority being the North Pole, and intimacy being the South Pole. The art of living consists in getting the balance between both just right. If not, then disturbances at the bottom invariably suggest a previous disturbance at the top, since the top precedes the bottom *in the temporal order*, but not in the spatial; the issue of authority always precedes that of intimacy *in time*.

The common denominator between authority and intimacy is *submission*; the latter is associated with letting go of your ego, separating from your desires and allowing yourself to be vulnerable. In order to discover your own authority, you first must submit to another's. In order to discover intimacy, you first must submit to another. In both instances, you begin by moving away from yourself. This is a universal teaching in religion.

Of course, religion assumes that the person is an adult who can afford to risk moving in this direction in the first place; it assumes a certain level of maturity. Psychologists, by contrast and for the most part, work with the immature. Their focus is on building the person's ego, putting them in touch with their desires, and encouraging them to be strong in order to deal with the dangers of this world. 'Submission' is not usually part of a psychologist's vocabulary.

The trouble is that too many immature people misunderstand the guidance supplied by psychologists; they begin to believe that *life itself* is all about 'empowerment', 'taking control', 'trusting your own experience', 'pursuing happiness', 'becoming free', 'moving towards your own goals' and all the other truths of psychology as preached in the very individualistic United States. They are like swimmers who go to the gymnasium for weight-lifting exercises to build up their strength, and end up believing that swimmers are weight lifters! In short, the immature can't tell the difference between the means and the end. Their mistaken belief is further reinforced when certain misguided psychologists begin to present their theories as a religion – as is the case with the New Age Movement.

It is for these reasons that I focused on the religious concepts of submission, separating, distancing, becoming impersonal and social to counteract the many D.I.Y. psychological concepts currently in circulation. Gordon W. Allport, in his introduction to Lewin's *Resolving Social Conflicts,* stated as much when he wrote, *"Without knowledge of, and obedience to, the laws of human nature in group settings, democracy cannot succeed"*; it is not just knowing the laws but of *submitting* to them through obedience that matters.

And perhaps a final conclusion to draw from this chapter is that, ultimately, the abused who desire that society should listen to them might model what society should do – listen by 'obeying the laws of human nature in group settings'. In short, let go of society and its abuser and show both what obedience and listening really mean – submission to the Higher Power, the ultimate protector of all children.

CONCLUSION

1. The Question of Evil

The term *good* originally came from - and is associated with - the term *gather*; mother is always good simply because she is the one who brings all together. In this sense, coming together is good, and staying apart is bad.

Curiously, when it comes to religion, things seem to go into reverse. The term *holy* refers to that which is transcendent, distant and apart (e.g. The Hebrews were a people who had been set apart from all others), and devotion to God implies a certain focus on separation. On the other hand, the opposite of devotion is addiction. And addiction - like the *evil* it is - always implies an *attachment*. And since the man in the family was always apart in the sense that he worked outside the house, then men became associated with religion and its apartness, while women became associated with family, community and the themes of togetherness. Men symbolise the distant Deity who is Holy and Mysterious (*Elohim*), women symbolise the God who is Close, Good and Personal (*Yahweh*); both symbolise different aspects of the same God.

Counselling as we know it puts emphasis on the *feminine* characteristics of gathering, understanding, becoming personal and intimate with another. It fosters the movement towards 'getting to grips' with that which has to be grasped in order to bring it close.

By contrast, *trauma counselling* operates almost entirely on the *masculine* principles of separation and apartness that are necessary to keep evil - and addictions - at bay. In other words, while it might be 'bad' to be apart from *the person* who is 'good' for you, it is wise to keep yourself apart from *evil things* that could harm you.

This becomes particularly true with the evil of child sexual abuse. Evil really does attach, and the major problem with this form of abuse is that it certainly attaches the so-called 'victim' to evil – even to the extent that the 'victim' and 'it' become as one. That's because the child truly believes that s/he *caused* the other person to do evil things.

Let me re-state this in a different way; adults who were sexually abused as children tend to view themselves as evil. From this core belief flows a series of consequences that reflect their secret fears:

1. The child-like will be terrified of you discovering their 'secret', namely, that they have a magical power which can make you act in weird and evil ways!
2. They will be terrified lest you will see how they and evil have become one; accordingly they will seek to reassure you that their early life was 'wonderful'.
3. They will fall back on moral terms such as *coward* and *fool* to distract you from their very personal *'evil'*.
4. They will make use of certain symbols that remind them of the original evil; these take the form of symbolic things that later act as 'triggers'.
5. They will believe that the world would be a better place if they (and their 'evil') were gone from it. In other words, it is important for the trauma counsellor to realise that the abused really believe that **they are evil in their person**, and that each has a secret longing to be dead so as to clean up the world! This is

a sobering reality and not a figment of speech.

All of the above themes associated with evil come together to make up the power-struggle between you and your client. Of course, the latter will *not tell* you that he or she is evil as such; rather, they will attempt to demonstrate it indirectly – so that you can see it for yourself. In other words, they will casually describe the 'evil things' they've done in their life, not so much to shock you as to illustrate how 'evil' they really are! What they say is not as important as what they are not saying – namely, that when doing what they described, **they were evil in their person.** I cannot stress this point sufficiently. It is a belief that has gripped the person to the point of becoming an obsession; *"The Satan and I are as One!"*

Your job, in turn, is to oppose this tendency of the abused to blame, put a curse on themselves for what happened, or engage in self-fulfilling prophecies or self-mutilation.

2. The Community Response.

I began this book by referring to my years as a teacher in the Black West Side ghettoes of Chicago ('black', as I said before, was the politically correct term used at the time by those living in the neighbourhood). I also worked as a parish curate in the same area. Although truth to tell, the work was mostly social and youth directed. It was also during the U.S. Civil Rights era, and black Chicago was not exactly like London or Dublin at the time. Rather it was a place full of personal and social disturbance associated with the question, *"What does it mean to be black in a white society?"* And while most people focused on the social issues, black therapists had to face black clients with problems.

Those problems were many. In fact, a pastor in a nearby parish to ours kept a sign upon his wall that read, *"In this place, we aim for relative failure as opposed to absolute!"* This, of course, was in the days before the terms *Post*

Trauma Stress Disorder had been coined; nobody appeared to link the strange behaviour of the people with the consequences of slavery.

The chief problem for the white community at the time was that it had a low level of tolerance for those with a non-white skin. The chief problem for the black community was that it too had a low level of tolerance for those with a non-white skin. In other words, the low level of tolerance for non-whites was shared by *everybody* in the social world, be they black, white or any other colour! (Malcom X tried to convince black people that they actually were non-white, and not just white people with a sun tan as was a commonly held belief in the ghettoes at the time! For example, if you asked a white and black child to draw a man, both would draw a white man without thinking; 'The Man' was always white.)

Indeed, I recall having been at a group discussion of black teens where they were recalling their experiences of the media. One lad remembered the first time he say a black face on T.V. According to him, he became excited and yelled out, *"Hey, ma! Come in here! There's one of your people on T.V.!"* In other words, the individual child saw himself as precisely that – an individual (colourless) but one living in a black family. From this and from a multitude of similar instances, I tend to conclude that *how the majority view a minority is how individuals in the minority will view the rest of that minority.*

Given that the so-called racial problem was not so much a white or black one but, rather, a social one that affected everyone, black therapists were quick to realise that they could not function in the ghettoes without becoming social activists themselves; the problems that black clients raised in therapy were not their own, but had their origins in the social world itself, one that was dominated by 'white people', that is to say, by European-minded people living in

America who were unable to root themselves fully in its Constitution - together with Afro-Americans who, in having lost their roots, thought that they too had once been European – which many had been (Muhammad Ali, for example, had an ancestor from Co. Clare). This being the case, the only way for therapists to work was to change the environment that had created such problems in the first place.

As the black population in our district was then, so now are adults in this country who were sexually abused as children. All have been traumatised by events in the past, yet have to live with the consequences in the present. Each individual who was formerly abused thinks of him/herself as just another person, but views other abused adults in precisely the same way that society looks at them – as people to be handled with 'sensitivity and compassion' rather than as people who **witnessed a crime**. To be associated with such 'needy' people is most certainly not in the individual's best interest. Accordingly, many go into hiding to avoid being labelled a social outcast. Like Afro-Americans in the '60s, they go through life working under the illusion that they are 'white' (Ghosts).

If so, then clearly there is a great need for society to *change its attitude and language* when dealing with those adults who experienced child sex abuse. Terms like, *'horrible', 'terrible', 'awful', 'dreadful', 'diabolical', 'inhuman', 'monstrous', 'horrific', 'absolutely shameful'* and *'victim'* only reflect the reactions of society to its own shadow; they do not reflect the experience of the abused child (to the latter, the experience was usually human but strange, weird, frightening and, for some, painful/pleasurable). If anything, the use of such language only increases the terror in the body of the untreated child-like who now begin to view their associates (and themselves) as *'horrible, terrible, awful victims'* (not witnesses). In short, such language only re-traumatises the abused. Not surprisingly, they begin to act-out such terminology as ghosts. And society-the-blind has not the slightest idea that *it is creating those ghosts* through its media and public announcements in the first place. Nor have the ghosts the slightest idea that they are acting-out the role of society's shadow side, or of the dark side of a necessary illusion (hence the 'dark side of the Force' in *Star Wars*).

It makes more sense for society to make use of the language of the traumatised (and of religion), and to simply say, *"Those children have been put through a living hell by some of us"*. For that is the first truth that society has to face before it can even begin to consider change.

The second truth is that there is always the hope of resurrection; it is always better to light candles than to curse the darkness. And when dealing with trauma, it is always advisable to focus on summer rather than on winter, on life rather than on death. Bringing life to others is the religious way. Preventing further deaths is the 'European Way' of psychologists and social workers.

It is not for me to tell others how to function. I can only say that I learned from those black therapists in Chicago. Over the subsequent years, I have spent as much time dealing with social and environmental problems as with traumatised clients in a one-to-one or group setting. Indeed, one of my reasons for writing this book was to share information about trauma and its treatment with both counsellors and the social world in the hope that the lot of the abused might be improved in some small way.

Likewise, it makes sense for everyone in the social world to consider how they might improve the lot of the abused in some manner. The un-born child may need protection in the future but, here-and-now, those who want to be born-again or to rise from *sheol* (the state of being dead, or 'hell' as we now call it) need a lot of social support. *Nobody rises from the dead by themselves or by their own power* (in the Scriptures, it says that God raised Jesus from the dead).

3. Final Review

To facilitate that rising, I focused initially on paradigms that I found useful in working out the difference between counselling and trauma counselling. I then tried to show how *dangerous* is the application of counselling principles in certain group settings, be they encounter groups either for Prisoners Of War in Korea, or for Religious groups in California. I did this to highlight the danger in misunderstanding Rogers' core characteristic of *genuineness* in a helper, while adopting his one-sided and exclusive doctrine on *intimacy*; this combination can lead to non-judgemental therapists becoming abusive in the counselling situation as we saw happening in California. My purpose in highlighting such dangers was, not just to illustrate immoral behaviour among those seeking 'goodness', but to show the need for a more balanced approach when dealing with both in counselling; intimacy needs to be balanced by authority, just as following your 'true inner self' or conscience needs to be balanced by a sense of its social consequences (hence the 'informed' conscience).

Having pointed out the need for counsellors to balance intimacy with the minor theme of authority when working with regular clients, I then moved to the need for balancing authority with the minor theme of intimacy when working with traumatised clients. In short, trauma work requires *a reversal* of the principles that counsellors normally use.

To introduce trauma work, I preceded it with the chapter on *The Impersonal,* placing emphasis on the masculine dimension (as opposed to the feminine that is behind counselling). This is because trauma counsellors deal with the issue of *evil*. And when it comes to this, men come into their own. I say this because research in Social Psychology suggests that, while women are better than men in recognizing what is good, men are better than women in detecting evil. For example, if a couple fall in love, it is the women in the village who know it first, but if a car salesman is crooked, it is the male customer who senses it first. This does not mean that the sexes are unequal. Rather, it suggests that each complements the other, a necessity when raising an infant; the latter needs to be surrounded by goodness – the role of mother – while both need to be protected from outside evil, the role of father.

It is unfortunate that society embraced Rogers' theories about 'being true to your inner self' or being genuine, while adopting his Gospel of Intimacy. The latter rejected authority while the former rejected the idea of playing a role in society. The result is, not only that we are now in an increasingly secular society where many seek that which is good for themselves, and where there is no such thing as evil, but also where the down-grading of *roles* is fast leading us towards social anarchy. After all, we are now equal when it comes to messing up the planet.

It has taken trauma to waken everyone to the reality of evil in its different forms (tsunamis, hurricanes, melting polar caps, wars in the Middle East, drugs, alcoholism, rising house prices due to greed posing as a market-place, starvation and aids spreading in Africa due to neglect, child sex abuse at home by those imitating their social betters who pursue power etc). Accordingly, I moved from the need for the Impersonal into Trauma Work itself, touching on both the medical symptoms and on my own psychological approach to treating the abused. And as you will have noticed, my approach is entirely social in orientation, not personal as in regular counselling.

I work from the assumption that the client, who was once

abused by an agent from the social world, now views that world as the enemy. Furthermore, and when faced by that same world, the client does not know what *role* to adopt. This leads the abused to turn to the impersonal characters of the fairytale (the Ghosts of Christmas Past) as role models; the latter can be Little Red Riding Hood one moment, and Wolf the next. Or she can be Dorothy the Lost on a yellow-brick road and suddenly switch to a character with no brain (Strawman), no heart (Tin Man) or no courage (Cowardly Lion) etc. Accordingly, when she meets the impersonal Wizard of Oz (Trauma Counsellor), she tries out every role in his presence – leaving the counsellor as baffled as she, the client, was when abused. The cry of the abused is not just, *"I want my mummy!"* it is also that of the Ghost, *"I want to go home!"*

Given that the client seems to feel at home in some form of magical theatre, I as therapist join in the drama. It is not that I play the part of counsellor as such. Rather, I adopt the basic paradigm of Priest and, impersonally, play the part of 'Mother' in the opening acts, 'Wizard' in Act 2, 'Prince Charming' in Act 3, 'King' in Act 4 and so forth. And all the time while 'acting', I use the client as my Director.

Sometimes I get it wrong, and the Director will roar at me; some even get up and storm out of the counselling room in a raging huff! But later they return after they've cooled down. I always accept my responsibility for getting it wrong, and before long, the rehearsal continues as normal. And, of course, I try to be as impersonal and anonymous as any good actor – for the simple reason that the impersonal is always magical to a child. It takes a magician to make one person vanish and another appear in his place - which, if you think about it - and as I indicated earlier - is precisely what happens on a stage once an actor adopts a persona and becomes impersonal; it's magic!

I next looked at the props that act as a background to

the entire play – the social props of *hope, wisdom, heroism and humility*. Without these, 'the show can't go on!'

Finally, I rounded it all up by noting that the abused client appears to work unconsciously out of the over-riding paradigm of Ghost – even if this is not too clear in their struggles to communicate through fairytales with the adult that is you. Still, the message of the fairytale and of the Ghost is the same, *"You too will live happily ever-after if you are good"*. Especially when you can trust yourself to let go and forgive.

In other words, I work at the same level as a traumatised client, that is to say, at the level of a child – as surely as when counselling non-traumatised clients I worked at their level, that of an adult. The move from counsellor to trauma counsellor may seem like a move in an alternative direction (like moving from Rugby to Soccer), but the truth is that the move is merely a *reversal*; it is a move backwards from adulthood to childhood. As I said in the Preface of this book, it is a different *orientation*.

It does, however take a certain humility on your part as counsellor to make such a move. More importantly, it takes a lot of humility to *submit* yourself to further training before you go anywhere near the traumatised, training which you most certainly will require.

But eventually when you see a terrified child come out of hiding and grow up into a beautiful and mature adult, it will all be worthwhile. At that moment you will experience a marvellous sense of wonder at witnessing the birth of something new - the butterfly emerging from its trauma cocoon. Call it a rising from the dead if you like. Better still, call it hope for the rest of the world.

Perhaps you, the reader of *Counselling, Trauma and Religion*, are now in a better position to understand why.

APPENDIX 1

U.S. PRISONERS OF THE KOREAN WAR

In 1959, a private lecture was delivered by a psychiatrist at Great Lakes Naval Base to a group of seminarians. The topic dealt with what had happened to U.S. soldiers in prison camps run by the Chinese during the Korean War. I was a member of the class in attendance and, at the time, recorded in writing what had been said.

Subsequently, I found a small booklet on the same topic in Chicago's De Paul University Bookshop. It presented essentially the same material – but included the reference to 'Colonel Meyers' of whom I had heard no mention at the original lecture. As I recall, the booklet had been issued as part of a *'Freedom Forum Series'*, presumably issued by an anti-war group, and one that preferred anonymity at the commencement of the Vietnam War.

Neither the original lecture nor the booklet made any reference *to the number* of returning soldiers who had been interviewed in the Tokyo Hospital. But both lecture and booklet were consistent in their descriptions of what had happened to those men in the prison camps. In short, both supplied identical conclusions that had been drawn from the evidence available at the time, but neither supplied too much evidence, clearly for the sake of brevity.

Subsequently, I have learned that individual military

survivors of those prison camps later wrote personal accounts of how they had been tortured by their Chinese guards. But whether such accounts were written as a response to the original account or not I cannot say. In short, what I wrote in this book was honest, but whether or not it was the full story I will leave for others to decide.

APPENDIX 2

POLITICAL CORRECTNESS

An historian once said,
  "The trouble with those who wrote in the past is that
  they did not know they were writing in the past".
The trouble for me when writing about my past experiences
on Chicago's West Side was my poor memory. For that
reason, I referred to a book that I'd previously written
about them. Unfortunately back in 1970, I failed to realise
that I was writing in the past; I thought I was writing in the
present!

  Being 'politically correct' before the idea became
fashionable, I referred to the people in my neighbourhood
as 'black' since that was the 'politically correct' term among
the young adults with whom I worked; we ran a coffee-shop
– *"The Black Lite"* - on the West Side from '68 to '70. And
just before I left, I typed out my recollections and
impressions of what had been discussed – quite heatedly at
times – by those seeking to understand what it meant to be
black in a white society, and of my experiences with some of
them on the last Civil Rights March, *'The Poor People's*
Campaign' in Washington, 1968. I called the book, *"The*
Black Lite" for obvious reasons.

  I never published it, mostly out of respect for those young
men and women who had put their trust in me; the

material was just too personal and revealing. To me, it sufficed that the memories would not be forgotten.

When writing this current book, I found myself caught in a dilemma. Should I use the more recent politically correct 'Afro-American' when speaking about those in the past, or use the politically correct 'Black' of another era? I'm afraid that loyalty to my former friends took precedence over current political correctness. For that reason I used the term 'Black' but tried to balance it by making partial use of the term 'Afro-American'. Since no offence was intended, I trust none will be taken.

BIBLIOGRAPHY

Bettelheim, B: *The Uses of Enchantment*; Penguin, 1976.

Blocher, D.H: *Developmental Counselling*; The Ronald PressCompany, NY, 1966.

Bloom, S. L: *Creating Sanctuary; Towards the Evolution of Sane Societies*; Routledge, NY & London, 1997.

Bowlby, J: *Attachment and Loss, Vol 11. Separation: Anxiety and Anger*. Penguin Books, 1978.

Breger, L: *From Instinct to Identity*; Prentice-Hall 1974.

Carey, JW: *Communication as Culture* Studies; Unwin Hyman, 1989.

Carkhuff, R.R: *The Development of Human Resources*; Holt, Rinehart & Winston, 1971.

Carkhuff, R.R: *Helping and Human Relations*; Vol.1 & 2, Holt, Rinehart and Winston, Inc. 1969

Crossan, JD: *The Dark Interval: Towards a Theology of Story*; Argus Communications, 1975.

Deaux, K – Wrightman, LS: *Social Psychology in the 80's*, 4th Ed: Brooks/Cole Publishing Co, Monterey, Ca., 1984.

Douglas, M; *Natural Symbols: Explorations in Cosmology*; Random House, Pantheon Books. NY. 1970.

Egan, G: *You & Me; The Skills of Communicating and Relating to Others*; Brooks/Cole Publishing Co, Monterey, California. 1977.

Egan, G: *The Skilled Helper*; Monterey, Ca., Brooks/Cole, 1975.

Egan, G: *Face to face: The small-group experience and interpersonal growth*. Monterey, Ca., Brooks/Cole, 1973.

Eliade, M: *The Sacred and The Profane; the Nature of Religion*; A Harvest Book, Harcourt, Brace & World Inc. NY, 1959.

Eliade, M: *The Myth of the Eternal Return*; Princeton University Press, 1991.

Eliade, M; *Patterns in Comparative Religion*; University of Nebraska Press, Bison Books, 1996.

Herman, J. L: *Trauma and Recovery*. Basic Books (A division of Harper Collins Publishers), 1992.

Jourard, S.M: *The transparent self* (Rev. ed.); NY, Van Nostrand Reinhold, 1971.

Lewin, K: *Resolving social conflicts; selected papers on group dynamics*. Gertrude Lewin (ed.). NY: Harper & Row, 1948.

Maslow, A.H: *Toward a Psychology of Being*. Princeton. Van Nostrand, 1962.

May, R: *The Cry for Myth*; Souvenir Press (E&A) Ltd. London, 1993.

Menninger, K: *Whatever Became of Sin*; London. Hodder & Stoughton, 1975.

Mc Creave, E: *The Black Lite*; unpublished, 1970.

Pfeiffer & Jones: *Annual Handbook for Group Facilitators*, 1972.

Rogers, C.R: *Counselling and Psychotherapy*; Houghton Mifflin Co, Boston, 1942.

Rogers, C.R, and Wallen, J: *Counseling with the Returned Serviceman*; McGraw-Hill, NY, 1946.

Rogers, C.R: *Client-Centered Therapy*; Houghton Mifflin, NY, 1951.

Rogers, C.R: *On Becoming a Person*; Constable London, 1961.

Rogers, C.R. ed.: *The Therapeutic Relationship and its impact: A study of Psychotherapy with Schizophrenics*. Madison: University of Wisconsin Press, 1967.

Rogers, C.R: *On encounter groups*; NY, Harper & Row, 1970.

Rogers, C.R: *Toward a more human science of the person*;

unpublished paper, Center for Studies of the Person, La Jolla, Ca.

Stanislavski, C: *Building a Character*; Methuen Drama, 1992.

Thorne, B: *Carl Rogers*; Sage, 1992.

Van der Kolk, B: *Psychological Trauma*; American Psychiatric Press Inc, 1987.

ARTICLES and ALTERNATIVE PUBLICATIONS

http://www.ewtn.com/library/PRIESTS/LATINM.TXT provided me with The Story of a Repentant Psychologist - that of Dr. William Coulson – which I used in this book.

Post Traumatic Stress Disorder in the Royal Navy and its Management; ENB Course 812 Seminar, May, 1994. Royal Naval Hospital, Gosport, Hampshire. Unpublished.

The Sky before the Storm; a Wider Circle publication; 2004. Email: info@widercircle.org   www.widercircle.org